*f***P**

Also by Robert D. Novak

The Reagan Revolution
(with Rowland Evans)

Nixon in the White House: The Frustration of Power
(with Rowland Evans)

Lyndon B. Johnson: The Exercise of Power
(with Rowland Evans)

The Agony of the GOP, 1964

COMPLETING
THE
REVOLUTION

A Vision for Victory in 2000

ROBERT D. NOVAK

THE FREE PRESS
New York London Sidney Singapore

THE FREE PRESS
A Division of Simon & Schuster Inc.
1230 Avenue of the Americas
New York, NY 10020

THE FREE PRESS and colophon are trademarks
of Simon & Schuster Inc.

Designed by Deirdre C. Amthor

Manufactured in the United States of America

10 9 8 7 6 5 4 3 2 1

Library of Congress Cataloging-in-Publication Data
is available

ISBN 0-684-82746-8

For Eric Breindel
(1955–1998)

Contents

Society

Power

PART THREE
TOWARD VICTORY

Preface

On the wall of my office is a photograph of me with Haley Barbour, then chairman of the Republican National Committee, at the 1996 Republican National Convention in San Diego. It is autographed by Barbour with this inscription: "Best wishes to Bob Novak. Whose TV charm is exceeded only by his partisan loyalty."

That was typical political sarcasm. "TV charm" referred to the fact that my partner, Rowland Evans, and I had just given Barbour a hard time about Republican election prospects in an interview broadcast on CNN. "Partisan loyalty" referred to the fact that I, after forty-two years as a registered Republican, had re-registered as a Democrat so that I could vote in that party's primary in the heavily Democratic District of Columbia, having recently moved from Maryland to the capital city.

The point is that I am in no way a spokesman for—or, at this writing, even a member of—the Republican party. Some GOP leaders do not understand this. In 1998, a Republican leader in Congress telephoned me to complain about my criticism of the party leadership. "The trouble with you, Bob," he said, "is that you're so used to tackling the ball carrier when the Democrats had the ball that you're still tackling the ball carrier even though he's a Republican now. Bob, you're tackling your own team." I responded: "I've got news for you. I'm not on your team."

Indeed I'm not. Although I usually vote for Republicans, I have never voted a straight party-line ticket in any election and have voted for two Democratic presidential nominees. I have never contributed a dime to the Republican party; I now decline invitations to address their gatherings; and I have never, as a Washington journalist since 1957, been offered a job in politics.

So since my connections with the Republican party are tenuous at best, what right do I have to preach to the GOP? Because I am an American citizen, a journalist, and a conservative who has been on a steady trip to the right through my adult life. For all its failings, the Republican party is the only practical vehicle of conservatism in American politics, and in this book I offer one private individual's critique of how well it fulfills that role today and could improve, for the mutual benefit of the party and the nation.

This is my first book in eighteen years and my first book in thirty-four years written without Rowland Evans as my collaborator. It is also a departure from my previous four books, all of which were essentially reportorial. I still consider myself a reporter by profession, but most people, I suppose, consider me a commentator—partly because of my *Chicago Sun-Times* newspaper column but mainly because of my appearances on CNN as a highly opinionated talking head. This book is in my "CNN voice," the voice I also use in talking to friends, associates, and friendly adversaries.

The ideas expressed here were formed by a life looking at politics and journalism. They were shaped by conversations from 1958 through 1964 with Michael Bernstein, the chief

Republican counsel of the Senate Labor Committee, which amounted to a running conservative tutorial. Arthur Laffer and Jude Wanniski were my tutors in supply-side theory, and Wanniski has been generous with his sage counsel over many other matters for the past twenty years. In recent years, Lawrence Hunter and Stephen Moore were helpful in explaining to me the intricacies of many government programs. But none of them, of course, is responsible for my highly personal—if not idiosyncratic—worldview.

It is no exaggeration to say that this book never would have been published were it not for my insightful and persistent editor at The Free Press, Paul Golob. He is really much more of a collaborator than an editor. I thank my long-time agent, Esther Newberg, for putting me in touch with The Free Press.

I thank my friend and son-in-law, Christopher Caldwell, for reading my manuscript and for his many helpful suggestions.

My reporter, Stefanie Hohn, was indispensable in research and fact checking for my book. My assistants, Lisa Makson and Michele Stember, helped me produce and transmit the various drafts. Bernadette Malone, chief writer of the *Evans & Novak Political Report,* was always helpful with information and insights. On this as on all other projects, my office manager, Kathleen Connolly, kept me relatively organized.

PART ONE

The Republicans
in Retreat

The Surrender of '98

Was it really a "revolution" in 1994 when Republicans gained control of Congress for the first time in forty years? It certainly was more than a mere changing of the guard, with one political party taking power from another. Rather, this was a conscious attempt to change the way America had been governed for the past sixty years and, indeed, the way Americans lived. And the Republican takeover did have revolutionary characteristics: a wave of excitement, a fervent belief and hope that the world will be transformed.

But the true test of a revolution is what happens after the revolutionaries storm the gates of the palace and seize power. Do they live up to their ideals, or do they succumb to the trappings of the old regime? Do they remain united, or do they form factions and turn their weapons on one another? And if the revolution collapses, does it go out with a bang or a whimper?

The "Gingrich revolution" has all too quickly reached that critical point where these questions must be answered. The revolutionary spirit of 1994, symbolized by the Contract with America, is but a faint memory as the Republicans face the 2000 election in danger of losing their third consecutive presidential election and of losing their majorities in Congress as well. If the Republicans are to regain the upper hand in politics and are to create a political environment in which their most cherished principles can flourish, the time to act is now.

For the past five years, I have waited for the Republican party to use its congressional majority to institute a true conservative program in line with the promises made in the election campaigns of 1994, 1996, and 1998. But time after time I have been disappointed. Some conservatives—mostly at the grass-roots level but a few in positions of power—have taken their disappointment so much to heart that they have begun talking about abandoning the GOP itself and starting a new political party. Others are following Pat Buchanan into the Reform Party to advocate protectionist and anti-immigration policies.

This surely is a road to oblivion. First, it is an admission of defeat, and I am not yet ready to concede the battle is lost. Second, it presumes that ideological purity is more important than electoral success, whereas I think that a strong Republican party that embraces conservatism can still command a majority in the country in a way that a third party never could. And third, it does not really address the overriding problem: It is impossible to govern the country effectively from Capitol Hill. To make a true mark on the country's political culture, a party has to control the White House, as the Republicans did from 1981 to 1993, under Presidents Ronald Reagan and George Bush and as the Democrats have done under President Bill Clinton.

If the Republican party is to reach its potential as an engine of conservative reform, it must embrace its own principles—despite the discomfort this may bring the congressional leadership—and it needs to articulate a true vision for victory in 2000. Otherwise, conservatives should brace themselves for four more years of Democratic rule and significant changes in the way Americans live.

• • •

The Republican revolution truly ran out of steam in October 1998. In the first two weeks of that month, Speaker of the House Newt Gingrich and Senate Majority Leader Trent Lott decided to accept President Clinton's version of a catchall spending bill rather than risk a confrontation that might shut down the government just three weeks before the November midterm elections.

On the surface, it might seem that the president held the weaker cards. Facing the humiliation of impeachment proceedings in the House Judiciary Committee, Clinton did not command a majority in either house of Congress. Actually, Gingrich and Lott were the desperate ones.

The congressional leaders had one overarching desire: to adjourn the Congress as quickly as possible, so that the members could campaign for reelection and thereby stave off humiliating defeat at the polls. For the first time in the nation's history, it seemed possible that the party in control of the White House might regain control of at least one house of Congress from the opposition through a midterm election victory in the sixth year of a presidency.

These leaders remembered well the experience of the winter of 1995–1996, when the Republican Congress let the government be shut down, only to see the president turn this principled stand on its head, portraying the GOP as callous villains and creating a landmark political victory for himself.

Three years later, the Republicans had yet to recover from this massive body blow and were skittish about provoking the president again.

And so, in the fall of 1998, with the president riding high in the public opinion polls, Gingrich and Lott chose surrender over principle. During the course of the congressional session, the two leaders made no effort to pass individual appropriations bills (any of which might have been vetoed by the president), choosing instead to pack everything into a single 3,000-page omnibus bill, in the hope that they could sneak all of their spending provisions past the president. They refused to recognize that Clinton would not hesitate to wield his veto pen. When the president challenged them point-blank in October, the specter of a government shutdown was too much for them.

Rather than force the point, they backed down. First went any hope of tax cuts. Then Congress agreed to spend $29 billion out of the first budget surplus in a generation to cover "emergency" spending, which in reality covered spending that was anticipated far in advance (for the military occupation of Bosnia) and was required by statute (mandatory veterans' benefits). Clinton got much of the funding he wanted for additional school spending, while the Republicans dropped their call to permit people to use tax-free savings for private and parochial schools below the college level.

Even worse, tucked away in those 3,000 pages were hidden goodies, intended to help the president and his party in the election only three weeks away. Seeking to firm up Democratic support against impeachment in the House, Clinton made sure that any compromise budget would appeal to his minority and feminist constituencies. Black farmers were subsidized for their anti-discrimination lawsuits against the Agriculture Department. A contraceptive program for health insurance companies contained no "conscience clause" for doctors who opposed abortion. Worst of all, these clauses were included without a peep of protest from Gingrich or Lott.

Indeed, the two congressional leaders were not even permitted the dignity of negotiating directly with the president. While Bill Clinton spent September and early October helping to raise money for Democratic congressional candidates, he delegated four senior staffers to deal with the Speaker of the House and the Senate majority leader. "I don't think the president is anxious to see the Republicans after all they've said about him," said one Clinton adviser. Although Gingrich and Lott fumed over this flagrant show of disrespect, it didn't seem to have stiffened their spines. The president knew that they would do anything to get out of town. And they did.

The capitulation of the Republican congressional leadership did not go unnoticed by others in the party. Jack Kemp, the former congressman, cabinet secretary, and vice-presidential candidate, had grown increasingly critical of the leadership shown by his friend and ally, Newt Gingrich. On October 8, on the eve of the budget surrender, Kemp issued an extraordinarily harsh statement about the congressional leadership, most of them his longtime political allies and former colleagues. "Today, the Republican Party is adrift," he wrote, "without an agenda and without purpose beyond its seeming preoccupation with saving the Congressional seats of its incumbents."

Kemp was particularly critical of the failure of the Republican Congress to deal with the high level of taxation.

Twenty years earlier, when he was in Congress, Kemp had been a lone voice calling for tax relief, and it was his Kemp-Roth tax bill that had formed the basis of Ronald Reagan's massive tax cuts in 1981. Kemp noted acidly in his statement that although Republican candidates across the country were campaigning for tax cuts, the leadership on Capitol Hill had not even tried to pass tax cut legislation, and he warned that "voters may think a political party whose leaders are unwilling to risk losing a vote on principle once it is in office is unworthy of winning the next election."

This was a view shared by many of Gingrich's colleagues in Congress and especially by the Republican rank and file beyond the Capital Beltway. Robert Bennett, the veteran Republican state chairman of Ohio, was a professional party man who was not especially ideological and was loath to criticize the elected leadership of his party. But two weeks before the November 3 election, he was blunt. He told me: "The Republican leadership in Washington for the last two weeks has not been helpful to Republicans campaigning in the hinterlands. We badly need tax cuts on the table."

In private, Bennett and his fellow state Republican leaders were even more scathing about the party's leaders on Capitol Hill. Some even speculated darkly that the Speaker of the House might not keep his lofty office for a third term after this election. It was a far cry from the heady days of 1994 when Newt Gingrich was the visionary leader who had generated a political earthquake. And as the year 2000 and the next presidential election loomed, Republicans around the country began to wonder what was to be the fate of the Grand Old Party.

•   •   •

From the Civil War to the Jazz Age, the Republican party was the dominant force in American politics. Republican candidates won fourteen of the eighteen presidential elections from 1860 to 1928, and the Republicans controlled at least one house of Congress for sixty of the seventy years from 1861 to 1931. The long Republican hegemony ended with the Great Depression, as the Democrats won control of the House in the 1930 election and two years later took over the Senate and the presidency under Franklin D. Roosevelt's New Deal.

Not until 1946 did the Republicans regain their congressional majorities, and then they were able to hold them for only two years. General Dwight D. Eisenhower's landslide victory for president in 1952 carried with it a Republican Congress, but it too lasted only two years. Despite Republican presidential victories in 1956, 1968, 1972, 1980, 1984, and 1988, Democrats still controlled Congress—forty uninterrupted years of House majorities and thirty-four years of Senate majorities, broken only by the Republican Senate of 1981–1987. After the Democratic landslide in the recession year of 1958, the Republicans most often were a puny, and increasingly ineffective, minority.

The Democratic ascendancy on Capitol Hill meant more and bigger government: higher taxes, tighter regulation, increased spending. President Ronald Reagan proclaimed a "revolution" in 1980, but even he could not reverse the trend toward big government, while reducing marginal tax rates. And when Bill Clinton defeated George Bush in 1992 and took office with solid Democratic majorities in both the House and the Senate, it appeared that the GOP had been brought to its knees.

But in the flush of victory, Clinton committed a series of costly mistakes. Elected with a plurality but not a majority of the popular vote, he felt he needed to shore up his base among the liberal Democrats—and failed to recognize how such measures might cost him support among voters in the center. To satisfy a key Democratic constituency, he made his first policy initiative to open the armed services to homosexuals. This served to strain relations not only with the military brass but also with large segments of the electorate. Then he put his wife, Hillary Rodham Clinton, in charge of devising a big-government plan to overhaul the national health care system. It was too much for the American people to swallow, and by the autumn of 1994, health care was a dead issue.

Unbowed by defeat, Clinton's chief political strategists were determined to make that year's congressional election a national referendum on health care. "We'll just beat the Republicans like a piece of bad meat," promised Clinton political adviser Paul Begala, invoking the vernacular of his native Texas. In most years, congresssional elections tend to be fought out over local issues, not national ones, but the administration was determined to nationalize and coordinate the Democratic effort.

The election of 1994 was indeed nationalized, but in ways the White House never envisioned, thanks mainly to perhaps the most mercurial of national political leaders, Newt Gingrich. An eight-term congressman from the suburbs of Atlanta, Gingrich had been an undistinguished history professor at Georgia State University before his election to the House in 1978. He had run twice previously, in 1974 and 1976, on a moderately liberal Republican platform emphasizing civil rights and environmental issues. It was only after moving to the right in 1978 that he turned the corner, and he entered the House as a firebrand, chafing at the passivity of his party's leadership.

By the time of Gingrich's election, the Republicans had been in the minority for a quarter of a century, and their leader, John J. Rhodes of Arizona, was nonconfrontational toward the Democratic majority. In 1981, Rhodes retired and was succeeded by Robert H. Michel of Illinois, who if anything was even more deferential to the opposition. Like most of their GOP colleagues, they represented safe Republican districts and seemed perfectly content with Democratic rule in Congress. Michel was a frequent golf partner of Democratic Speaker Thomas P. (Tip) O'Neill, and after he left Congress, he often mourned the loss of bipartisan bonhomie. (When Michel faced an unusually strong labor-Democratic threat in his Peoria, Illinois, district in 1982, O'Neill privately expressed concern over the possibility that his good friend Bob might be defeated.)

From his first day in Congress, Gingrich railed against the Rhodes-Michel mentality and sought to lay the groundwork for a Republican majority. If he had to make Capitol Hill a less friendly place, so be it. Gingrich saw his opportunity in 1989, when he charged Democratic Speaker Jim Wright with corruption in connection with a questionable book deal. In lieu of paying an honorarium for speaking engagements, the Teamsters union, an oil lobbyist, a Fort Worth land developer, a liberal Texas insurance entrepreneur, and a Boston-based insurance company purchased, by the thousands, bulk copies of Wright's 117-page paperback, *Reflections of a Public Man* (a collection of his speeches and anecdotes assembled by a congressional aide on the public payroll). The Speaker received royalties far above the usual scale, in effect, laundering money though his royalty account. At first standing almost alone against the House's ethos of collegiality, Gingrich forced Wright from office in

1989 and in the process harvested poisonous resentment toward him from the Democratic side of the aisle.

To the astonishment of even his own friends, later that year Gingrich was elected—by a single vote and against Bob Michel's opposition—to replace Dick Cheney as House Republican whip, the second-ranking position in the party leadership. Cheney, a conservative and former chief of staff to President Gerald Ford who was well liked and respected on both sides of the aisle, had resigned to become secretary of defense under President George Bush. Gingrich could not have been more different from Cheney in his approach to the job. He did not care whether the Democrats liked him; he was a partisan warrior who sought the ultimate goal of a Republican takeover of power—under his leadership.

In 1994 his moment came. Gingrich made clear that whatever the outcome of that year's congressional elections, he would challenge Bob Michel for the House Republican leadership. At age seventy-one, Michel had no stomach for a bitter intraparty battle and announced that he would retire at the end of the congressional session. There was no opponent against Gingrich to succeed Michel.

In preparing for the fall election campaign, Gingrich launched an audacious venture: a "Contract with America," pledging a vote within the first hundred days of the new Congress in 1995 on ten issues, including tax cuts, welfare reform, regulatory and tort reform, anti-crime measures, the line-item veto, term limits, and a balanced budget. The Contract with America provided a framework for Republican unity in a nonpresidential election year, especially after more than three hundred Republican congressional candidates gathered on the steps of the Capitol on September 27, 1994, to sign the document and pledge to uphold its provisions if elected.

"This year's election offers the chance," the preamble stated, "to bring the House a new majority that will transform the way Congress works. That historic change would end government that is too big, too intrusive, and too easy with the public's money. It can be the beginning of a Congress that respects the values and shares the faith of the American family." United by the Contract, appealing to a growing anti-Clinton reaction in the country that had mobilized Christian conservatives, gun owners, and term-limits advocates, the GOP picked up an astonishing gain of fifty-four seats in the House and nine in the Senate. Newt Gingrich, improbably, was Speaker of the House, the third-ranking official in the U.S. government.

As 1995 began, the optimism within the GOP ranks was infectious, but disillusionment with Gingrich soon set in, as the indefatigable opposition leader and far-seeing visionary turned out to be an ineffective, mistake-prone leader of the congressional majority. His first mistake was to sign a $4.5 million book contract with HarperCollins, prompting speculation that Gingrich was trying to enrich himself at the public's expense and that he was now beholden to media tycoon Rupert Murdoch, the owner of HarperCollins. Although Gingrich restructured the contract so that he received only standard royalties and no advance, the controversy emboldened the Democrats and the press. It was a turning point, and by midyear the Republican revolution was stalled.

The conventional wisdom of why the soaring hopes of the 104th Congress crashed is that the Republicans underestimated the tactics and toughness of Bill Clinton, particularly in the government shutdown at the end of 1995. Clinton twice vetoed Republican bills, forcing the offices of the government to be closed and "nonessential" employees to be sent home. The new House majority whip, Tom DeLay, wanted the Republicans to outwait Clinton, but Gingrich could not withstand the abuse the Republicans were getting in the news media. Clinton put the blame on Congress, and Congress capitulated and made a budget deal on the president's terms. The Republicans never recovered from that retreat.

The Republicans had been so sure of victory that they had no contingency plans for defeat. "We were committed to the idea of Clinton as a weak president who would ultimately feel required to sign an agreement with us for a balanced budget with tax cuts," Gingrich later admitted. When Clinton didn't turn out to be so weak, the Republicans found themselves out on a limb with no way to climb back.

All that was true, but much more was involved as well. For all of the Republican esprit de corps during the first hundred days in 1995, there was a tension from the start within the Republican ranks. The bright-eyed amateurs elected in the GOP sweep of 1994 sincerely wanted to change the way business was done on Capitol Hill. But the old hands in Congress (particularly in the House), who had waited so long to taste the fruits of victory, were not about to dismantle the system that the Democrats had enjoyed for forty years. The metaphor I like to use is whether the Republicans would close down the executive washroom or merely change the locks. They opted to change the locks.

One early test of principle involved a mundane congressional perquisite. At overcrowded Washington National Airport (hopelessly obsolete before its remodeling in 1998), parking spaces were at a premium. During rush hours, the regular parking lots and a single parking garage were always filled. But next to the main terminal was a large lot that was never more than half-filled and often was three-quarters empty. Its sign explained why: "RESERVED FOR MEMBERS OF CONGRESS, SUPREME COURT JUSTICES, AND DIPLOMATS." The Supreme Court and diplomatic listings were window dressing. This was a parking lot for congressmen, and it meant a lot to them as they hurried to make their weekend flights home.

Why, it was asked, should these elected representatives of the people be entitled to this special privilege? Many of the newly elected freshmen of the class of '94 asked that question, and so did a very small number of their more senior colleagues. But the Republican leaders laughed off the question. Only the sign was changed. The new sign read simply: "RESERVED."

That symbolized the determination by the Republican leadership to run Congress very much as the Democrats had. Above all, they were not going to make a great effort to enact campaign finance reforms that would curtail the flood of lobbyist contributions. And as long as the lobbyists could contribute large sums of money to congressional campaigns, there wouldn't be any meaningful tax reform either.

The most important betrayal of principle by the Republicans in Congress was their deception on term limits. The party had gladly accepted the contributions and the votes of the term-limits movement in 1994, but actually liked the idea no better than the Democrats did. Indeed, the tip-off came even before the 104th Congress convened, when the new House majority leader, Dick Armey, mused that the Republican takeover had rendered term limits unnecessary. The Old Bulls of the House GOP were professional politicians who had no desire to give up their seats after a few terms, and with surprising speed, many of the freshman Republicans lost the stars in their eyes too. Membership in Congress was too enjoyable and too rewarding to be sacrificed. It was not surprising, then, that the only item from the Contract with America to fail on the House floor was the proposed term-limits legislation.

While some members of the class of '94, like Thomas Coburn of Oklahoma, Matt Salmon of Arizona, and Helen Chenoweth of Idaho, sincerely believe in term limits and will retire from Congress after the 2000 election (much to the consternation of the Republican leadership), others have been less principled.

The poster child for term-limits hypocrisy in 2000 is George Nethercutt of Spokane, Washington, who in 1994 defeated the sitting Speaker of the House, Thomas S. Foley, primarily on the term-limits issue. Nethercutt's pledge to serve no more than three terms was a marked contrast to Foley's thirty-year tenure in the House and to the Speaker's unpopular lawsuit in which he had sued the people of the state of Washington for approving term limits in a referendum.

But Nethercutt was at heart a creature of Washington, D.C., rather than the state of Washington. He was a lawyer who had long labored in the nation's capital as a congressional aide, and it soon became clear that he was not going to honor his term-limits pledge. In 1999, he announced that he would run for a fourth term in 2000, prompting the organization U.S. Term Limits to mount a vigorous advertising campaign against him in Spokane.

House roll calls told the larger story. Tom Coburn and the other House members who adhered to their term-limits promises were dependable votes for smaller government and lower taxes. The George Nethercutts of the GOP were markedly less dependable.

• • •

By all historical precedents, the Republicans should have lost their congressional majority in 1996, repeating the party's history of controlling Congress for only two years at a time, as was the case in 1947–1948 and 1953–1954. Bill Clinton was racing to an easy victory over Bob Dole in the presidential race, and the momentum was clearly with the Democrats.

What intervened was the late-breaking scandal that the Democrats had raised millions of dollars through illicit campaign contributions from Asia. The scandal was enough to slice into Clinton's margin of victory and to salvage the Republican majority in the House—but just barely. The GOP majority fell from fifteen to nine seats.

The 105th Congress convened in a far different mood from its predecessor. The freshmen from the class of '94 who had entered Congress as starry-eyed members of Newt's army were now cynical sophomores who blamed the Speaker for the party's loss of momentum. Gingrich's position was made even shakier by the fact that he was under an ethical cloud on a variety of dubious charges that he had converted public funds for personal use, charges lodged by Democrats who had never forgiven him for forcing Jim Wright from public life and were thirsting for retribution. No charge was proved, and years later the Internal Revenue Service, very quietly, cleared him of tax-evasion charges. He did sign an incorrect disclosure statement prepared by his lawyer and agreed to pay a $300,000 fine and to apologize to the full House in the opening days of the session in January 1997. He won reelection to a second term as Speaker by the narrowest of margins, with nine Republicans joining Democrats in voting against him.

By the late spring of 1997, Gingrich's hand-picked leadership team, headed by Majority Leader Armey, was in rebellion. These rebels included the party's brightest rising light, forty-three-year-old Representative Bill Paxon of Buffalo, New York. A Gingrich protégé, Paxon had headed the Republican congressional campaign committee's masterful operations in 1994 and had been appointed by the Speaker to a new post, chairman of the leadership. Paxon soon became a favorite of the freshmen; he was conservative though not confrontational, a skilled politician though still an idealist.

In early July, a band of insurgents, mostly from the class of '94 but including some more senior members as well, determined that Gingrich had to go. Majority Whip Tom DeLay met with the rebels and then with Armey, Paxon, and John Boehner, the chairman of the House Republican Conference (who ranked fourth in the party's House hierarchy, behind Gingrich, Armey, and DeLay). The leaders agreed that Armey would replace Gingrich as Speaker and that Paxon would be the new majority leader.

But when DeLay reported back to the other conspirators, he met unexpected resistance. Tom Coburn asserted that the backbenchers' choice as Speaker was not Armey but Paxon. DeLay was stunned. He left the room and informed his fellow leaders of Coburn's remarks, which effectively drove Armey to the other side and ended the coup attempt. A few days later, Armey told his colleagues that it would be "immoral" to move against Gingrich, and he proceeded to warn the Speaker of the threat to his leadership.

That was the end of the coup, but not of the disruption. Paxon admitted his complicity and resigned from the leadership, after being told that that was Gingrich's wish. DeLay made a similar admission but stayed in the leadership. Armey denied everything, and Boehner said nothing (guaranteeing that efforts would be made to dislodge both of them from their positions in the next session of Congress—unsuccessfully against Armey, successfully against Boehner).

Gingrich was safe for now, but Republican wounds had been opened. And when the second session of the 105th Congress began in January 1998, the Speaker was no longer his fiery self.

Survival was now his keyword. To avoid the confrontations of the past, Gingrich was determined only to suffocate President Clinton's legislation. He was confident that even if the Congress accomplished nothing positive, the Republicans would nonetheless be saved by the historical precedent of the "six-year itch," whereby the president's party always lost seats in Congress, usually a lot of them, after six years in office. Gingrich resolved to do absolutely nothing as he waited for the November election, while attacking Clinton over the burgeoning scandal over the president's affair with a young White House intern named Monica Lewinsky.

But despite Gingrich's plan, it is an iron law of politics that Congress must do something, and in 1998 that something turned out to be a lot more spending. With the concurrence of the Republican leadership, an immense highway bill was passed, despite the protests and opposition of young insurgents like Lindsey Graham of South Carolina and veteran legislators like John Kasich of Ohio, the chairman of the House Budget Committee.

By the time the session ended with the Surrender of '98, the radicals were bitter and laid down the law. If the Republicans failed to gain at least ten House seats in the midterm elections, they said, Gingrich was in trouble. And if the unimaginable happened and the Republicans actually lost seats in the face of the six-year itch, Gingrich was finished. The

Speaker was untroubled. After all, his advisers had told him that with Clinton on the road to impeachment, a gain of twenty seats was not just possible but likely. November 3 couldn't come soon enough for him.

•   •   •

It was a paradox. William Jefferson Clinton was about to be impeached, but he achieved what no other president had accomplished since 1822 (when President James Monroe's Era of Good Feelings constituted virtual one-party rule): his party actually gained seats in the House of Representatives after six years in office. When the new 106th Congress would convene in January 1999, the Republican majority would be trimmed to a razor-thin five seats. The diagnosis of the debacle was universally accepted. There had been no Republican agenda in the 105th Congress, and Newt Gingrich was to blame.

The end came swiftly. Representative Robert L. Livingston of Louisiana, whom Gingrich had promoted in 1995 over three more senior members to become chairman of the House Appropriations Committee, showed his gratitude by announcing his candidacy for Speaker. Livingston represented a departure, but it was questionable whether he was pointed in the right direction. He was certainly no ideologue, and he was even less an aggressive champion of the private sector than Gingrich. For the previous four years, he had been primarily devoted to preserving the interests of the "appropriators," those congressmen in charge of spending the public's money. But the backbench rebels supported him anyway, for one very important reason: he was not Gingrich. Bill Paxon had had not sought reelection in 1998 and retired from politics at the early age of forty-four. Livingston was all the rebels had.

Livingston did not have the votes to defeat Gingrich in the Republican conference, but the unique nature of the speakership proved Gingrich's downfall. Unlike the majority leader and the whip, the Speaker is elected by the full House, not just by his party, and there were enough Republican dissidents who said they would join with the Democrats to deny Gingrich the majority he would need to remain as Speaker. To be sure, intense pressure would be placed on those dissenters to support Gingrich in the House election, but such a process would be ugly, dispiriting, and ruinous for the Republican future. And so Gingrich did the right thing. Before the week was out, he resigned from Congress, leaving Livingston an open path.

The path, however, did not remain open for long. Larry Flynt, the publisher of the pornographic magazine *Hustler,* revealed the existence of adulterous affairs in Livingston's past, and Livingston stunned the House during a Saturday morning debate on Clinton's impeachment by announcing his resignation from Congress. By midafternoon, the Republicans had lined up behind a new heir apparent: J. Dennis Hastert of Illinois, a former high school wrestling coach who had served unobtrusively in the House for six terms and had never held elective leadership office. He was currently serving as chief deputy whip, the principal lieutenant of Tom DeLay (who played a major role in easing Livingston out and Hastert in), and had made many friends and no enemies within the party. He was hailed as a competent, nonabrasive legislative mechanic.

Denny Hastert, the unexpected Speaker, came into office pledging to make the trains run on time. And that posed a major conflict going into the 2000 election. Apart from the unfortunate reference to Benito Mussolini, whose early apologists asserted that at least the Italian Fascist dictator made the trains run on time, the desire to adhere to a tight legislative schedule was bred in the Republicans' fear of failure deriving from the shutdown of '95.

Compromises on spending and other issues quickly became apparent as the Hastert era began. Except for a serious effort to cut taxes in the summer of 1999 (though the tax-cutting bill, vetoed by Clinton, was seriously flawed), there was not much more of an agenda than there had been in the preceding three years under Gingrich. Significantly, most appropriations bills continued to be crafted to bring bipartisan agreement and thereby avoid a session-end logjam. Obscured by Democratic complaints of draconian spending cuts, spending continued to rise inexorably.

Actually the train schedule was a little chaotic. In an effort to get the spending bills passed on time, the Republican leadership was keeping the House in session late into the evening—past ten o'clock, eleven o'clock, or even midnight. At the end of July when routinely asking Majority Leader Armey in a colloquy on the House floor for the next week's schedule, Democratic Caucus chairman Martin Frost asked if it might be possible to require a curfew similar to the restriction that Philadelphia and other cities once imposed on baseball teams that no inning could start after 11 P.M. Armey was not amused. In midsummer 1999, a resentful Bob Livingston was telling former colleagues that if he were Speaker, the House would be quitting at a decent hour each night.

• • •

As the 1999 congressional session progressed, it seemed that the agenda was being set more by the minority Democrats than by the majority Republicans. After two students at Columbine High School in Littleton, Colorado, shot to death thirteen of their fellow students and then killed themselves, the Democrats demanded new gun control legislation. There were no convincing arguments that the proposed new regulations—safety locks or restrictions on sales at gun shows—could have prevented the Littleton tragedy. Indeed, some twenty existing gun laws had been broken by the high school killers. Nevertheless, polls showed a public demand, echoed by individual Columbine students, to prevent future carnage.

So when Senator Edward M. Kennedy requested a full-scale debate on gun controls, Majority Leader Lott agreed. That triggered a sequence of events leading to the passage of an unexpectedly restrictive gun control measure (with Vice President Al Gore, the probable Democratic presidential for 2000, casting the vote as president of the Senate to break a tie). A bipartisan coalition in the House later blocked the panicky ride to passage, but the Senate proceedings showed Republican leaders unable to keep their rank and file loyal to the gun owners, a major element in the coalition, and ineffective in controlling the flow of what was happening on the Senate floor. It was a familiar story of GOP fecklessness over the past five years.

The combination of Democratic determination also forced action on reform of health maintenance organizations and campaign finance, with Republican leaders kicking and screaming rather than shaping the issues to their liking. Except for the sole issue of tax reduction, the Republican leaders were trying to run out the clock in 1999, for surely nothing would be accomplished in the election year of 2000.

The great Republican accomplishment of 1999 was the passage in late July of a large, but flawed, tax cut bill. Yet instead of following normal procedure and sending the bill immediately to President Clinton, who was expected to veto it, Republican leaders held it back as Congress adjourned for the month of August. Seeking to keep Clinton from trashing the bill while Republican members of Congress were scattered around the globe during the recess, the GOP leadership planned to sing the praises of their bill across the nation. By the time the lawmakers reconvened on September 8, they calculated, Clinton might feel constrained to sign the bill or at least negotiate a compromise.

It didn't work out that way. Some Republicans tried to promote the tax bill to their constituents (especially Speaker Hastert), but many others were abroad on junkets or resting at home. Polls showed that Americans, enjoying a prosperous economy, gave tax-cutting a low priority (though many other surveys showed that voters, logically enough, would welcome lower taxes). When the lawmakers returned after Labor Day, the Democrats eagerly awaited the battle while the Republicans seemed timid and uncertain.

On September, 8, Senate Majority Leader Lott abruptly and surprisingly announced that there would be no attempt to resurrect the tax bill once Clinton vetoed it. Nobody was more surprised than Speaker Hastert, who had contemplated a post-veto revival with a compromise bill that would join a major package of tax cuts with a Clinton-sponsored minimum wage increase. But Lott and Hastert had not conferred during the long summer recess and had not bothered to schedule a meeting for their first week back in Washington. Rather than protest and trigger news stories of internal Republican dissension, the Speaker yielded.

The stunning absence of a Lott-Hastert meeting also meant the absence of a session-ending budget strategy, as Republicans lurched toward possible repetition of the surrender of 1998. Unwilling to risk another government shutdown, the congressional leadership could avoid another catchall omnibus bill only by meeting the president's spending demands on individual bills.

The attention of the congressional leaders, like that of Republicans elsewhere, was not on the forlorn hopes of crafting a real agenda on Capitol Hill but on George Walker Bush, the governor of Texas. All hopes were pinned on a rookie in national politics, anointed by the party establishment as its choice long before the first primary was even near. The confirmation of that anointment was Bush's phenomenal money raising. By mid-July 1999, he had collected a record $38 million in individual, $1,000-a-crack contributions. By October the figure was an astounding $60 million, with much more to come.

Bush had the endorsements and the money, was likable and attractive, and had run very well in Texas with minority groups and women, who had hurt Republicans badly in the previous two elections. But could the son of President George Bush be counted on to carry out the party's revolutionary impulses, or would he follow his father in disastrous compromises?

Whatever the answer to that question, the early anointment rankled conservative Republicans also seeking the presidential nomination. Senator Bob Smith of New Hampshire dropped his presidential bid and left the party. Much more menacing to Republican prospects, Patrick J. Buchanan prepared to bolt and run as a third party candidate. But beyond disgruntled also-rans, many Republicans wondered whether the party elders were wise in putting all their money on an untried candidate whose position on the Republican agenda was uncertain.

What agenda? Going into the 2000 presidential election, this is the state of the Republican agenda as crafted on Capitol Hill:

- No consensus and no real action on tax reform
- Tax reduction scaled down with only a small portion of the projected budget surplus dedicated to lower taxes and legislation cluttered with special interest plums
- Dismantling of government agencies set aside
- Acceptance of the federal government's current scope and power
- Abandonment of the term-limits cause
- The movement against abortion and racial quotas set aside
- A leading federal role in education and health care accepted
- An uncertain trumpet on foreign affairs and defense

This looks suspiciously like the me-too Republicanism of the post–World War II generation—the Eisenhower administration's "dime-store New Deal," in Barry Goldwater's memorable description. It was a failure the first time around, starting when Republican presidential nominee Thomas E. Dewey walked away from the major accomplishments of the Republican 80th Congress on his way to an unexpected defeat in 1948. The subsequent election triumphs of Dwight Eisenhower and Richard Nixon continued the watered-down, copy-cat facsimiles of Democratic policies that served mainly to suppress the growth of the Republican party.

The congressional wing of the party for the most part has admitted that only the election of a Republican president in 2000 can advance a more imaginative agenda. In October, 1999, they held their tongues while Bush consciously separated himself from the unpopular Capitol Hill GOP. They are content to sit on the sidelines until such a president is elected. The stakes could not be higher, yet the foundation is shaky as the fate of the revolution awaits the election of 2000.

Controlling Congress
Is Not Enough

Tom DeLay is a smart man, a straight shooter, one of the more effective congressmen I have seen in over forty years in Washington. While as majority whip he was number three in the House Republican hierarchy, he was the kingmaker who engineered the elevation of Dennis Hastert to the Speaker's chair. Indeed, privately many colleagues considered him the most powerful member of the House of Representatives. Particularly skilled in backroom maneuver and pressure, he did not get where he was without knowing a lot about how the game of politics is played in Washington.

Yet in the summer of 1998, DeLay told me that he felt if he had a choice of which branch of government to control, he would take Congress over the presidency—take it in a heartbeat without looking back. I think he's totally wrong and that this attitude is part of the reason the Republicans find themselves in a precarious state going into the 2000 election.

It used to be said of the French general staff that they always fought the current war as if it were the last war. Politicians tend to respond to confrontation in much the same way. And in the case of DeLay and the other Republicans who took power in the revolution of 1994, the "last war" was the confrontation between the two Georges from 1989 to 1992—when Senate Majority Leader George Mitchell, who became the maximum Democrat of his era, repeatedly took the initiative away from President George Bush. Mitchell's most important achievement was to force the notorious tax increase in 1990, maneuvering Bush into breaking his "read my lips—no new taxes" pledge from the 1988 campaign.

Nobody had expected such a virtuoso performance from George Mitchell when he was elected Democratic leader in 1988, after the election that put George Bush in the White House. A Republican was president, but the Republicans were in the minority in both houses of Congress. A soft-spoken former federal judge from Maine, the newly elected majority leader immediately went one-on-one with the newly elected president. The Mitchell style was best exemplified by the way he handled three issues in which he absolutely overwhelmed Bush.

First is capital gains tax cuts—one of the few promises of Bush in 1988, during a campaign that was long on image and short on policy. This was an issue that tended to unify Republicans while many Democrats from the South, farm districts, and the timber-growing Northwest deserted their party's nominee, Michael Dukakis, and backed George Bush's position. Passage looked like a cinch. But Mitchell never gave in. The White House thought Mitchell was trying to compromise; in fact, he wanted to kill the proposal. Bush retreated steadily. Finally, by the end of 1989, the issue died. It was suffocated partly by Bush's caution, partly by hostility from the Senate Republican leader, Robert J. Dole, but mostly by Mitchell's determination, including threats of a filibuster.

Second, Mitchell would not retreat from his determination to pass an affirmative action bill that amounted to racial preferences. Bush was opposed, and so was his staff. But Mitchell labeled the affirmative action bill as the Civil Rights Act of 1991. How could George Bush, a son of the New England upper class and the longtime contributor to the United Negro College Fund, oppose a "civil rights bill"? He had always regretted coming out against the 1964 civil rights act while he was making an unsuccessful bid for the Senate on a Republican ticket headed by Barry Goldwater, and he was not going to do it again as president twenty-seven years later. To the consternation of conservative White House staffers aides, Mitchell won and Bush lost. The Republican president had backed a Democratic quota bill.

Third, and by far most important, were the protracted budget negotiations of 1990. As Bush reneged on his capital gains promise, he simultaneously retreated from his 1988 "read-my-lips" pledge. Mitchell was relentless in the endless budget sessions at Andrews Air Force Base, insisting that there absolutely had to be a tax increase and that there could be no more spending cuts. Little by little, Bush consented to the breaking of his pledge. The Republican president backed a Democratic tax-increasing budget. The tax increase in the midst of a recession, unrelieved by a drop in capital gains rates, guaranteed that Bush would be a one-term president.

In the eyes of the Republican revolutionaries of 1994, George Bush's weakness was misinterpreted to indicate that the executive branch had lost its power over the direction of government—a systemic shift since the days of the "imperial presidency" of the 1960s and early 1970s. But this shift really was due to the personalities of the individuals involved.

George Mitchell, skillfully managing the power of the

Senate, made himself the strongest majority leader since Lyndon B. Johnson in the late 1950s. Although he lacked Johnson's institutional control over the Senate, from the standpoint of achievements I would judge him as more effective than Johnson. The legend of Lyndon Johnson was that he always seemed to be in command, but I don't think he had nearly the success with Eisenhower that Mitchell had with Bush.

Mitchell might have been flattered when I wrote about him as the best majority leader since LBJ, but he really hated it when I called him the most partisan Senate leader ever. Mitchell liked to think of himself as prudent, fair, and judicial, but in fact he succeeded by being partisan to an extreme, not only in opposition to a Republican White House but also in pushing a Democratic agenda. As Republican Trent Lott began his first full year as majority leader after the 1996 election, he talked about playing George Mitchell to Clinton's George Bush. It didn't work. Lott was too nice a person to engage in rough-and-tumble partisanship, and there is probably no other president of the United States who ever truly reveled in partisan play as much as Clinton has.

Because Mitchell had a comfortable majority to work with—55–45 in the 101st Congress (elected 1988) and 56–44 in the 102nd Congress (elected 1990)—he was able to preach the old-time Democratic religion in pursuing a liberal agenda, which played well with the senators' constituencies back home. The Bush White House drifted onto the defensive.

Lyndon Johnson, by contrast, operated as majority leader by not having an agenda. In his first two Congresses, when the Democrats recaptured the Senate in 1954 and held on despite Eisenhower's reelection in 1956, he never enjoyed more than a two-seat majority. He felt that he needed to work with the Republican White House, not against it, if he was to get enough votes to maintain his authority over the Senate.

There are two big differences between what happened then and what was to come. One is that partisanship was less obvious in the 1950s, and political parties were much less homogeneous. Much of the Northeast was Republican but fairly liberal. The entire South was Democratic but very conservative. So you had a large conservative southern Democratic faction and a large liberal Republican faction. This makeup forced coalitions and militated against partisanship, and was a great advantage for President Dwight D. Eisenhower, whose legislative ambitions were limited at best. He entered politics to keep the United States in NATO and make the Republicans an international party both economically and diplomatically. Still, the presidency was clearly the dominating branch in setting policy, especially with the Congress so divided.

In this environment, Johnson maintained his leverage by never enunciating a clear agenda, which generated a great deal of criticism from the Democratic national chairman, Paul M. Butler, and from other liberals who wanted to confront Eisenhower. In answer to Butler, Johnson in 1956 issued a "Program with a Heart"—a collection of moderately liberal Democratic proposals. Not surprisingly, it didn't go anywhere, and LBJ was soon back to agenda-less leadership.

Johnson's tenure generally had more sizzle than substance in this very closely controlled Congress, yet he did get some things done. In 1955, he was highly effective in supporting the liberal decisions of the Supreme Court under

Chief Justice Earl Warren, which drew a lot of opposition from both sides of the aisle in the Senate. Perhaps a majority of senators wanted to reduce the Supreme Court's authority and override decisions that they saw as wrong-headed. But Johnson was able, through the use of parliamentary maneuver, to counter all of those proposals effectively. In 1956, he added disability payments to the Social Security system, which became the forerunner of Medicare. It was a brilliant job of maneuvering.

Johnson practiced public relations. I remember one time he called a routine Senate authorization of a couple of new vessels the Naval Modernization Act. In 1957, he passed the first civil rights bill since Reconstruction. It wasn't much of a bill; he gave away a lot, extracting all of the teeth to placate the southerners. But he passed it, and got credit for making a major stride forward in civil rights. That's what used to drive the liberals nuts. He would get all of these kudos for doing little things that really didn't change the status quo all that much. For the celebrated LBJ leadership, there wasn't all that much of a work product.

In 1958, everything changed. The Democrats won a huge victory in the midterm elections, gaining a thirty-seat Senate majority—an advantage of the magnitude that they would not relinquish until the Reagan landslide brought in a Republican Senate in 1980. In some ways, it was the worst thing that could have happened to Johnson, because now he had to have an agenda and couldn't rely any more on splitting the difference and winning praise for his deal making. Now that he had an agenda, he became much less effective as a legislator.

Congress began to be polarized as the country moved toward 1960 and an open election. The Democrats wouldn't have to face Eisenhower again, and the party wanted to present a strong platform going into the fall campaign. Paul Butler's attacks on Johnson intensified as he urged a totally oppositional role toward Eisenhower. But Johnson said he couldn't do that; he felt it wouldn't be good for the country.

Johnson (and his fellow Texan, friend, and mentor, House Speaker Sam Rayburn) still had to deal with that conservative southern bloc, which wasn't very sympathetic to the Democratic National Committee's agenda. And as a result, the liberal program that Johnson tried to put through in 1959 and 1960 was almost entirely blocked—a total failure—despite his huge majority.

Why? Because of the inherent power of the presidency and the improbable fact that Eisenhower awakened for the last two years of his second term. He suddenly got very interested in domestic matters and started vetoing legislation he did not approve of. Looking at it from a distance, I think you could say if anybody had any doubts about the inherent dominance of the executive branch, they should have been removed by the last two years of the Eisenhower presidency facing the big Democratic majority in Congress. The entire Democratic agenda—federal funding for Medicare, education, and various other domestic programs—went down to defeat, even as Eisenhower was able to push through passage of the Landrum-Griffin labor reform bill to tighten federal regulation of organized labor against the explicit opposition of the Democratic leadership in Congress.

Clearly the Mitchell-Bush model was the exception over the past half-century. But you couldn't tell that to Tom De-Lay and the Republican revolutionaries of 1994.

•   •   •

When the Republicans under Newt Gingrich were planning their strategy in 1993 and 1994, they forgot about Dwight D. Eisenhower and Lyndon B. Johnson, and remembered only how weak George Bush had been and how impotent Bill Clinton now seemed, especially after the fiascoes on gays in the military and on health care.

So the victorious Republicans said, "This guy is as weak as Bush, and we can kick him around." They didn't think they needed to plan a strategy to maintain their momentum after Election Day, and they weren't helped any by their leadership in the Senate.

On the morning after the 1994 elections gave them control of both houses of Congress for the first time in forty years, the new Senate majority leader, a surprised Bob Dole, had no plans for his newfound majority. When he was asked by CBS's Dan Rather about his "number one legislative priority," Dole replied, "There are a host of things that I think we can do to make the same laws apply to us that apply to small businesses or apply to CBS—whatever—make them apply to Congress." That was a laudable if somewhat banal goal, but hardly the first project that would occur to most leaders suddenly thrust into majority status.

Newt Gingrich was definitely not surprised and did have an agenda. The Contract with America was supposed to be the starting point of a "revolution" designed to cut down the scope of government. But what he loved far more than specific points of policy was his visionary overview of American politics. He took enormous pride in having gotten rid of the Democrats, feeling that it was his Contract with America that swept into power the first Republican majority in forty years.

Gingrich breached seniority on several committees to install his people in chairmanships, and he liked to envision himself as the most powerful Republican Speaker since the days of Uncle Joe Cannon at the turn of the twentieth century. It was all very exciting, but he was less excited—and really not all that effective—when it came to getting legislation passed.

Gingrich had an extremely short attention span, and he was visibly restless even before work on the Contract with America was completed. I had breakfast with him early in 1995, when rumors were flying that he would run for president in 1996. I asked him about the rumors and he said, "Well, don't you think I've done all I can do here?" I almost fainted, because he hadn't done anything.

His mind wandered. I think his mind-wandering is the only explanation for the HarperCollins controversy at the start of his speakership, which brought him immeasurable troubles from which he never really recovered.

Gingrich also fell victim to a common failing among politicians: a desire for the opulent lifestyle that their largest supporters enjoy. Politicians are put in contact with these people, going to their homes for fund raisers, meetings, and social events. Gingrich, an army brat and a college-professor-turned-politician, who always had lived from paycheck to paycheck, was envious of that life.

That is why so many former elected officials, once freed from the constraints of politics, can think of nothing but making money. That's what happened to Jack Kemp at the close of his twenty-five-year career in public service. Why does he need a seven figure annual income in speaking fees? The answer: he *thinks* he needs it. Other retired politicians get themselves appointed to corporate boards. Still more become lobbyists. It's the quest for uncounted wealth.

And so in January 1995, when HarperCollins came to

Gingrich with that $4.5 million contract offer, he thought that that was a hell of an idea. He never considered how it would look to the outside world to accept that kind of money from a company owned by Rupert Murdoch, one of America's great press lords. He never thought how it would undermine his standing as a "revolutionary."

Even one of Gingrich's allies, former Congressman Vin Weber, has told me that Gingrich probably should never have held a position in the House leadership higher than chairman of the congressional campaign committee. I think that's probably correct. Gingrich's great skill was in setting a pattern and strategy for winning elections, not in controlling the House of Representatives. It became obvious that he was a failure as Speaker—with grave implications for the Republican party.

•　•　•

Newt Gingrich's inability to lead the country from the Speaker's chair became painfully obvious during the fight with Bill Clinton at the end of 1995 that led to the government shutdown. It was in that showdown that Clinton reenergized his presidency and set himself on the path leading to his reelection the following year.

Gingrich has admitted that he and the rest of the leadership miscalculated by underestimating Clinton. What is even clearer is that they underestimated the presidency as well. Clinton discovered after the 1994 defeat that the presidency's bully pulpit could be used to beat the Republicans at their own game, and with the help of his brilliant and unconventional political consultant Dick Morris, he adopted an innovative four-headed strategy:

1. Adopt all the good stuff from the Republican platform that tested well in polls and focus groups. Everything was polled to see what would play in Peoria, and what came back was this list: fiscal responsibility, middle-class tax cuts, a balanced budget, smaller government, and welfare reform.

2. Knock the hell out of the Republicans any time Clinton could make them look mean. If Congress was proposing a smaller *increase* for the school lunch program than the Democrats were proposing, the Clinton-Morris team would portray the Republicans as taking bologna sandwiches out of the mouths of kids all over America. The GOP was painted as anti-poor, anti-old, anti-young, anti-women, anti–minority group, anti-gay, anti-everything.

3. "Bite-size" the programs that make ordinary people more dependent on the government. Can't swallow the big health care reform? Find something bite-sized. The American people were intuitively suspicious of big, overreaching government programs like the 1994 Clinton health plan, but when these programs were chopped into small parts, Americans swallowed them nicely. They felt that would provide them security without fear of government regimentation.

4. Buy advertising time all over the country to promote the president and his agenda, focusing on issues that tested well, issues that made the Republicans look mean, and issues that were bite-sized. Clinton and Morris also went directly to the people, under the media's radar, by buying ads everywhere except New York and Washington. This is why they needed so much money from China and all other points of

the compass. This also left the Republicans unsure of how best to respond to such tactics.

And so, as the congressional leaders were trying to negotiate with Clinton and trying to keep their powder dry for the 1996 election, they were hearing things back from their constituents who were seeing the Clinton commercials. Now the Republicans began to worry that they might lose control of Congress in 1996 and began to gear their efforts almost entirely toward the preservation of their majority in Congress.

If I may borrow a concept from Asia, the Republicans in 1995 lost the "Mandate of Heaven." Back in the days of the Vietnam War, I was told by worried Vietnamese citizens that there was a feeling in Saigon that because of the corruption of the regime, it had lost the Mandate of Heaven and therefore could no longer rule effectively.

The best way to translate the Mandate of Heaven into Western terms is to equate it with the concept of credibility. In the first months of the Republican Congress in 1995, the leadership began to abandon the cause of radical reform, which had been the bedrock of its popular support in the 1994 elections. They backed away from term limits, any kind of campaign-finance reform, the elimination of cabinet departments, the elimination of the National Endowment for the Arts and the Corporation for Public Broadcasting, their stance against affirmative action, and, of course, comprehensive tax reform, which started in 1995 as a shining light, only to fade further and further into a remote and undefined future.

In the budget negotiations that led to the government shutdown in the fall of 1995, Clinton knew that the public would interpret the shutdown as the fault of the "mean" Republicans. He built that concept through his early sub rosa media campaign. And so he wouldn't give in. He was very tough—far tougher than his adversaries had imagined he would be. The Republicans later complained that he was impossible to negotiate with and often lied to them about his intentions.

That may be correct, but the overriding truth is that House Majority leader Dick Armey and Republican National Committee chairman Haley Barbour had it right when they said that Gingrich should never have negotiated with Clinton; Congress should have just passed its own budget instead and not cared whether Clinton vetoed spending bills. The intimidating factor of sitting across from the president of the United States was just too much to avoid giving away things.

At one 1995 meeting of Republican leaders, Armey wrote on a piece of paper, "No summit conferences"—a reference to the summit conferences in the Bush administration where George Mitchell had dominated the agenda and had dominated George Bush. Barbour too had advised the Republicans that they weren't very good at negotiating and should stay away from Clinton. But this advice was ignored.

So just as the budget negotiations were dominated in 1990 by the legislative branch, they were dominated in 1995 by the executive branch. The Republicans finally submitted to Clinton; they ended the shutdown and accepted his terms. The effect was that it seemed as if the president had prevailed and the Republicans had been responsible for the shutdown. Now the shutdown did not really affect the lives of many Americans other than civil servants. But it became a symbol of Republican intransigence and insensitivity.

I believe that the most significant impact of the shutdown

was not that it changed public opinion so much, but that it changed the morale of the Republicans. They became very leery, very cautious about being able to make a comeback, particularly when they had so badly underestimated Clinton and the power of the presidency. In fact, the government shutdown so intimidated the Republicans with the fear that they would lose individual seats, and possibly their majority, that they backed away from a major tax reduction or major spending reduction for years to come.

• • •

Republican problems go deeper than simply having been outfoxed by Bill Clinton. For twenty-four years, from 1969 to 1993, the Republican party was the presidential party; its power derived from having four Republican presidents over that period. Most of the party's initiatives and brainpower originated in the executive branch. But since 1994, the Republicans have become a congressional party, which I think has changed the personality of the GOP, and in ways that party leaders never imagined.

In the Old Testament, after the Israelites left Egypt, they yearned for the fleshpots they had left behind. Similarly, the Republicans on the Hill became enamored of their own fleshpots—the pleasure of being in the majority, of having big staffs, of controlling the calendar, of the mechanical power of running the show. Goodness knows, the Democrats enjoyed it for forty years. Now the Republicans were enjoying it. Having changed the locks, they reveled in newfound access to the executive washroom. The thing they feared and dreaded most in all the world was to revert to minority status on Capitol Hill.

Unlike the Republicans who had wielded power through the executive branch under Nixon, Ford, Reagan, and Bush, many of the senior Republicans in Congress who came to power in 1994 were professional politicians who had spent much of their life in politics.

That's why term limits are such an underreported yet crucial aspect of the Republican problem. A self-term-limited member of Congress looked at things differently. It was a matter of in-and-out, not caring about the fleshpots. The term-limited members were more radical, more interested in issues, less worried about losing. These definitely were not the leaders of the congressional party.

In many ways, the people who served in Republican administrations in the 1970s and 1980s as cabinet officers or subcabinet officers were more like term-limited congressmen than the non-term-limited congressmen who controlled the party in the 1990s. George Shultz, for example, was a distinguished professor of economics who had not held high public office until he came into the Nixon administration as secretary of labor and later budget director and secretary of the treasury. He returned to the private sector as a business executive until 1982, when he was appointed by Ronald Reagan as secretary of state. Not being a professional politician didn't prevent him from becoming a dominant figure in two Republican administrations.

The first Eisenhower cabinet was called "ten millionaires and a plumber." Ike named one Democrat—Martin Durkin, a plumbers' union official—as secretary of labor; Durkin didn't last a year. Eisenhower brought in a real Republican businessman (though a moderately liberal one), Jim Mitchell, to replace Durkin. The Eisenhower cabinet members may have all been rich, but they were not professional politicians.

They were essentially businessmen and financiers, as was true to a great extent of all the Republican administrations since World War II.

It is possible to argue that at least the top elected Republican leaders in the House after 1994 were the kind of people you would think would be citizen legislators. Dick Armey and Newt Gingrich had come from academe; Tom DeLay had owned an exterminating company. They are not, on the surface, people who had spent their whole life in politics. But it did not take long for them to act like professional politicians. While the most stringent term-limit proposal of six years service in Congress is derided for being too short, perhaps it is too long. Enjoying the pleasures of leadership turns citizen-legislators into professional politicians all too soon.

There is something else. Many lesser-known Republican congressmen, not leaders but senior members of the Appropriations Committee who have been on the Hill a long time, had been in the minority throughout their congressional careers and had been intimidated and bossed around by the Democrats during those long years. And so the most important thing in their world was not getting rid of the National Endowment for the Arts or even scrapping the Internal Revenue Code. It was enjoying the fruits of being in the majority party. They didn't keep their eye on the ball.

Furthermore, exercising leadership in Congress is a very different task from leading the country, as the Republicans have discovered. Leading the Congress, whichever party is in power, is based on Sam Rayburn's maxim, "To get along, you go along." In other words, if you want to have any success here, don't be a rebel and don't cause trouble; you have to go along.

I think of Mark Neumann, who was elected to Congress

from Wisconsin in 1994, a young self-made millionaire who sold one of his home-building businesses to have the money to run for Congress. He was given a seat on the Appropriations Committee, a highly coveted assignment that is not often awarded to a freshman. Almost immediately, he voted against a defense appropriations bill because his own proposal to bar money for the U.S. military occupation of Bosnia—originally approved by the committee—had been removed from the final version of the measure. Neumann's vote violated one of the House's sternest taboos: Appropriations Committee members never vote against an appropriations bill.

Neumann's vote helped defeat the bill, a humiliating rebuff for Bob Livingston, the new Appropriations chairman. The hot-tempered Livingston had a fit. He tried to kick Neumann off the committee and was promptly faced with a full-scale revolt from Neumann's colleagues in the big and boisterous class of '94. Livingston had to be content with bumping Neumann from the important Defense subcommittee to make an example of him for the other freshmen. Neumann had a hard time with the House leadership from then on as he pressed for deeper cuts in government. In 1998, he ended up running for the U.S. Senate against the Democratic incumbent, Russell Feingold, a race he almost won.

Mark Neumann never liked the House, and the House leadership never liked him. He had the mistaken notion that he had been elected to Congress to make a revolution, and the party's leaders were aggressive in pointing out that misconception. He was not missed by the establishment.

I am not the first person to voice complaints about the Republican leadership in Congress. The cliché is that leading Congress is like herding cats; it's hard to get them to go anywhere together. But the GOP leaders don't even seem up to the far easier chore of herding cattle.

Nobody in the leadership since 1994 was terribly effective in putting forth a positive agenda. Dick Armey, a conservative professor of economics and a true believer in the free market, proved inefficient and incompetent as majority leader and had to fight hard against two competitors to be reelected after the 1998 election. It was held against him that he didn't level with people about his participation in the attempted coup against Newt Gingrich in 1997, for which Bill Paxon of New York, not Armey, paid the price for being booted out of the leadership. Tom DeLay was popular among the members as majority whip, particularly after he admitted his own participation in the failed 1997 conspiracy, but he was so intensely partisan that as Speaker he would be a lightning rod—Gingrich squared, in intensity—for attacks by the opposition and the news media that cannot abide him. A lot of people thought that Bob Livingston would have been really good as Speaker, but I'm dubious. As an appropriator, he was a huge spender with no inclination to downsize the government—with a bad temper to boot. After his active extracurricular sex life was revealed and he was eased out (with DeLay leading the easing), his quick replacement for the speakership was the nonconfrontational Dennis Hastert, whose top priority was decidedly not revolutionary: to bring order out of chaos in the House.

Leading the country is a different story. Haley Barbour said repeatedly in conversation (much to the consternation of Gingrich and his entourage) that you can't lead the country from Congress, and I agree. It was impossible in Eisenhower's day, and it's even more difficult now because of what *Washington Post* media critic Howard Kurtz has called the "spin cycle," mastered at the Clinton White House. The White House position is put out at the morning briefing and repeated endlessly during the day on CNN and on the other networks.

There is no such procedure—there is really no attempt at such a procedure—on the Hill. I often wonder that they don't even try to do something similar, but the truth is that it's probably just not doable. There is so much more of a controlled environment in the White House. In Congress, with 535 elected representatives of the people available for comment, if a reporter doesn't like what a particular congressman is saying (that is, if he thinks he's being "spun"), he can just go find somebody else who will give him a different story.

In this huge country, it's very hard to have a single congressional voice coming out and saying, "This is what we have to do," and mobilizing the country to action. Gingrich tried to be that voice, but his personality and his ego got in the way. He started off in January 1995 by having no-holds-barred, short press conferences on a regular schedule—at least one per week and maybe more. It was rough. The press was really hitting him hard. All of his advisers and colleagues said, "Don't do that; it's murder."

Gingrich's ego was such he didn't like to be bruised, and he went to the other extreme. He not only closed down the press conferences, but he made himself inaccessible to the news media. This was quite a change; Gingrich had always been one of the most accessible members of Congress. Even before he was elected in 1978, he used to call me or David Broder or one of the other columnists. When he first ran for Congress he said, "Whenever you go through Atlanta, I'm not far from the airport. I'll come out to see you between planes." Suddenly in power, he couldn't take the bruising, particularly when the book contract came up and the press started smashing him on it. I think if he had stuck with those regular press conferences, they would have been a very good starting device to help him lead the country to support the Republican agenda.

The problem of looking to Congress for national leaders brings me to Bob Dole. After 1994, the Republicans were trying to govern the country from Congress, and then in 1996 they nominated a man who had spent most of his adult life in Congress. A lot of what went wrong with Dole as a presidential candidate is directly attributable to his background as a congressional leader.

First, a little history. In this century, there have been only two sitting members of Congress who have been elected president, both of them senators—Warren G. Harding in 1920 and John F. Kennedy in 1960. It's hard to run for president from Congress, and it's hard to have the broad outlook that you probably need to do the job once elected. The Ronald Reagans and the Jimmy Carters and the Bill Clintons are distant from the seat of government, and tend to have a better outlook, I think, about what it takes to run for president. Even the typically Washington-type candidates—Johnson, Nixon, Bush (the elder)—did not run directly from the Senate or the House.

As far as Dole was concerned, it is true that even if he had been the governor of Kansas rather than a senator, he still would not have been an appreciably better candidate. I think he was just a very bad presidential candidate temperamentally. He ran four national campaigns, each one worse than the one before. He learned nothing. One of the silliest things that ever happened was the idea that he was going to resign from the Senate in 1996, which was going to make him "Bob Dole, private citizen from Russell, Kansas." Nonsense. He didn't go back to Kansas; he stayed in Washington (as do most members of Congress, which makes "They never go back to Pocatello!" one of the enduring clichés of American politics). No one ever believed that Dole was leaving Washington if he lost the race.

Bob Dole had the right personality for a Senate leader but the wrong personality to run for national office. He was a micromanager, a difficult person, easily peeved. As a senator, he was parochial in that his horizon often seemed bound by the walls of the Senate chamber. People who have spent their whole lives in the legislative arena tend to be parochial.

I remember one time in 1994, I was a guest at the City Club of Washington, where there must have been a hundred people gathered for breakfast to hear Dole, then the Senate minority leader, speak. Nearly all were lobbyists (I was the only journalist there, and I was the guest of a lobbyist). Without the benefit of notes, Dole went through every piece of legislation of any importance in the Senate, committee by committee. This was toward the beginning of the session, and he knowledgeably assessed each bill and its chances of passing—all the while offering very few value judgments about these proposals. It was an amazing tour de force. All these lobbyists were taking notes to send back to their clients and employers: "I had breakfast with Bob Dole this morning, and he gave me the lowdown on that bill we're interested in . . ."

Ronald Reagan could never have pulled that off. Ike couldn't have pulled it off. I doubt even Clinton could have pulled it off. But the hard truth is that having too many facts gets in the way of being an effective national leader. You have too many trees and can't see the forest. And that was a major part of Dole's problem in 1996.

One of Dole's predecessors as the Senate Republican leader, Everett McKinley Dirksen, went Dole one better. He not only could assess the status of every bill in the Senate; he actually knew the contents of every such measure—a fact that enormously enhanced his power in the Senate. In the horse trading that goes on in a legislature, knowing what's in every bill means you know what you can give up to get the most important things passed. However, such micro-knowledge can be ruinous for being a national leader; it's too much information. You can't break free.

What too many people in politics fail to recognize is that the presidency is not an administrative job. It's a leadership job, which is entirely different. It involves articulating a vision, pointing people in the direction you feel the country should go, inspiring people. It does not mean knowing what's in every clause of every bill. Eisenhower, based on his military experience, propagated the myth that he was actually running the government, but in reality he let the government run itself. Carter tried to micromanage and served only to prove that it can't be done. Clinton, no Eisenhower and certainly not a Carter, decided not even to have cabinet meetings.

• • •

As the 2000 presidential election draws closer, the news media will continue to focus on Washington, featuring members of Congress as spokesmen for the Republican party. This is not such a good thing for the GOP. The leadership in Congress is so snakebit, so terrified of losing their majority, that they have taken playing it safe to a pathological extreme. What they are saying is, "Okay, the best thing we can do is to do no harm. Don't have a government shutdown. Don't have confrontations where we end up losing. Don't have programs based on how much we cut the school lunch program. Do make the trains run on time. But put all your marbles on the presidency. And stay out of Clinton's way."

They're going to find that that strategy is a serious impediment. The Democrats are intensely partisan on Medicare, Social Security, and so many other issues. It's hard to stay out of their way. What this means in the end is that the Republican leadership in Washington will push the Republican agenda only so far, and that could become a recipe for defeat, no matter who is the presidential nominee, because it allows the Democrats to define the issues in their terms.

Staying out of the way is a typically mechanical, poll-driven, Washington idea, driven by fear, lack of confidence, lack of interest in pursuing goals. But another option was always open and might even be in 2000, notwithstanding the new cliché that nothing, absolutely nothing can get passed in an election year. Congress could identify attractive Republican issues and do something about them. They might not—probably would not—succeed in enacting many laws over Clinton's veto, but pursuing an agenda would show the country what the party stands for.

Nobody likes this tax system. Young people don't like it; lower-income people don't like it; minority groups don't like it. Congress has been playing around for better than fifty years talking about tax reform, and doing less and less about it. That's something the Republicans could tackle.

On Social Security, they could follow the lead of Pat Toomey, a new congressman from Pennsylvania with plausible proposals for making the first steps toward privatization. He's gotten nowhere, because the idea is dangerous. It opens the Republicans up to attack. If you propose something, after all, some people will be against it (especially if the White

House is against it), and you will get the full brunt of their attack.

The Republican Congress should have been courageously advancing the Republican agenda and should not have been afraid of it. But they're not playing to win; they're playing not to lose.

Nothing else captured this timidity so well as what happened in the wake of Bob Livingston's resignation as Speaker designate on December 19, 1998. I have made clear that I am not a Bob Livingston fan, but he was a very flamboyant personality, quite an imposing figure. Whether he would have been good or bad as Speaker will never be known, but he certainly would have been assertive in promoting a Republican agenda. With his sudden, unexpected resignation on a Saturday morning, the other congressional leaders were so insecure that they felt they had to have a replacement for Livingston before the sun set that day.

To repeat, Tom DeLay had convinced Livingston that he could not serve as Speaker, and now DeLay convinced others to back his deputy whip, Dennis Hastert, for the post. Support was lined up by two o'clock in the afternoon, just four hours later. What were the Republicans looking for? Not another Gingrich and not another Livingston. They were looking for a guy who would not cause trouble, not embarrass them, and would not have opposition. Denny Hastert is a fine gentleman and a dedicated public servant, but his selection was hardly a way to inspire confidence from the electorate.

What if, following Livingston's resignation, DeLay and his associates had taken some time to consider their options before naming a new speaker? What could have gone wrong?

At the least, it might have meant an election contest. At

the worst, it might have meant another Gingrich—an unstable visionary—and that was not what the party leadership wanted. But in fact, the alternatives were not all that frightening: Christopher Cox of California, a cerebral former Reagan aide with a broad grasp of policy; Steve Largent of Oklahoma, a dedicated but self-disciplined conservative representing the class of '94; James Talent of Missouri, well respected and hard working, who could combine intellectual integrity with backroom skills.

But all of these potential Speakers likely would have taken a confrontational stance toward the White House in Clinton's last two years, and the bulk of Republicans feared that this would have opened the Republicans to the outcome all feared the most: losing their majority. They agreed that playing it safe was the proper road to 2000. In so doing, they confirmed that controlling Congress is not enough for political domination in America.

Clintonized Republicans

No one can talk about what Bill Clinton has done to the presidency, and what he has done to the Republican party, without talking first about impeachment. I think that there has been complete confusion and misunderstanding when comparing the impeachment of Bill Clinton in 1998–1999 with the threatened impeachment of Richard Nixon in 1973–1974. The conventional wisdom is that Clinton's impeachment was a plotted conspiracy by the Republicans to get rid of a president they didn't like, whereas with Nixon there was a bipartisan response to a president out of control.

The reality is that the determination among the Democrats to destroy Nixon was very strong from the beginning, particularly from the left wing of the party. Representative Robert F. Drinan of Massachusetts, a Jesuit priest (later ordered out of Congress and out of politics, along with all other Catholic priests, by Pope John Paul II), typified and often led those who were determined to get rid of Nixon.

Drinan represented a substantial bloc of fire-eating liberals who were determined to remove Nixon from office but seemed less interested in the Watergate burglary than in the president's policies. Drinan's group wanted Representative Peter Rodino, chairman of the House Judiciary Committee, to use subpoena power to obtain documents and tape recordings pertaining to the bombing of Cambodia, the impoundment of social welfare appropriations, and other conservative acts of government that they considered impeachable. They pressured Rodino to issue "one-man subpoenas"—ordered by the chairman himself without consulting other members of the committee—and gave him the power to do so on a straight party-line vote in the committee. Rodino ultimately found enough substance in Watergate itself for an impeachment vote by the committee with some Republican support, but the process was anything but bipartisan and reflected long-simmering desires to remove Nixon from office on purely political grounds.

In contrast, I believe that, except for a very few members of Congress (most notably Representative Bob Barr of Georgia), there originally was little of such Republican fanaticism demanding Clinton's impeachment. Rather, it was an accidental succession of events that led to a course of action that only a handful of Republicans in Congress believed was going to be necessary or desirable when it began.

The congressional Republicans never really thought that the impeachment process would go as far as it did. I don't know anybody—Barr included—who at any time seriously thought that Clinton was going to be removed from office. What happened was that they got on a speeding bus that was out of control; they didn't know where it was heading and didn't know how the whole process was going to end. It was not a calculated political maneuver; in fact, they saw early on that they did not have public opinion on their side, but they felt they could not stop the process once it had begun.

The Republicans had no idea how to get off the runaway bus without doing even more political damage to themselves.

They recognized that most Americans did not like the process, which—in reaction to a calculated Clinton campaign—was widely seen as "unfair," and they wanted it to end as quickly as possible.

Nevertheless, the Republican base, which was already unhappy because of the agenda-less drift of the Republican Congress, was very unforgiving of the president and appalled at the thought that their elected representatives might be forgiving. Take the case of Representative Henry Hyde's district in the suburbs of Chicago. Polling data there published in Chicago newspapers indicated a great deal of opposition to the impeachment process, but the district's Republican base—the loyalists important to Hyde politically—would have been very disappointed if he didn't continue to pursue impeachment as chairman of the House Judiciary Committee. This pattern held true in congressional districts across the land.

I think there might have been random thoughts in the House, as the process went on, about how to get off the bus, but most thoughts went into how to make a better bus ride—more controlled, more comfortable, less dangerous. The worst-case scenario, everyone agreed, would have been to stop the process with a censure motion, which the Republicans felt would have been a distortion of the whole American system of checks and balances and would have weakened the institution of the presidency more than a full-blown impeachment trial would have done.

One congressional leader who wanted more than anything else to get off the bus was Senator Trent Lott. After the House voted to impeach Clinton, there ensued a running negotiation between Lott, the Senate majority leader, and Hyde, the chairman of the House Judiciary Committee, as to the nature of the Senate trial. How long it would last? Would there be witnesses? If so, how many? Would any such witnesses actually appear on the floor of the Senate? In short, would there be a real trial?

Trent Lott and Henry Hyde were old colleagues, dating from Lott's days in the House, usually bonded together as conservatives against the party's left wing. But on impeachment, they were on inexorably opposite courses. Since it was clear that Clinton never would be removed from office, Lott insisted on as little a trial as possible, violating all historical precedents.

So it was all negotiated and whittled down to the vestige of a trial, not a real trial at all. The whole process was very dispiriting to Hyde and the other House managers. In the end, they did get more than Lott wanted originally—which was no witnesses and a four-day trial. Instead, the trial lasted twenty-six days, most of it tied up in pro and con arguments and just long enough to go through the sham of deposing only three witnesses and showing the Senate condensed videotapes of their testimony.

The most important point here is that the Republicans let the process drive them rather than driving the process themselves. And this passivity is emblematic of how the GOP has responded to Bill Clinton throughout his presidency.

•   •   •

If I had to point to one part of the process that went particularly awry for the Republicans, it would have to be Independent Counsel Kenneth Starr's referral, in which he laid out the allegations against the president. Judge Starr was a fine appellate lawyer and is a decent man, contrary to the image of him in the mainstream media skillfully painted by the president and his friends. But as the independent counsel, he proved politically maladroit. On balance, I can't think of a worse outcome for all of this from the Republican standpoint than the way he handled it.

The Republicans in Congress expected a much broader-based referral that would get into allegations of presidential wrongdoing that were nonsexual in nature: the FBI files, Whitewater, the White House travel office—just anything beyond Monica Lewinsky. As it was, the referral was very limited in focusing exclusively on the Lewinsky allegations, and this played into the president's hands. The case for impeachment could be made by Clinton's defenders to appear as though there was just one indiscretion by the president instead of a pattern of misconduct on a broad spectrum of issues.

Right or wrong, failure to bring any action on the FBI files—"Filegate"—was the biggest disappointment for many Republicans in Congress. They suspected a plot that could be traced to the Oval Office regarding the murky circumstances under which confidential FBI files of prominent Republicans somehow were "discovered" at the White House in 1996. (Many Democrats had their suspicions as well.) The right-wing judicial activist Larry Klayman uncovered a great deal of information about the files scandal that could have added much more potency to Starr's referral, but the independent counsel seemed to lose interest in this set of disturbing facts.

And on the Whitewater land transactions, Starr's case collapsed as he lost one witness after another. Former Clinton business associate (and alleged paramour) Susan McDougal turned out to be uncooperative, preferring imprisonment on contempt-of-court charges. Her ex-husband, James McDougal, became most cooperative and convincing, but (as he had prophesied) he died in prison in 1998. David Hale, a former traffic court judge, was the star witness ready and willing to testify that both the president and his wife had broken the law in connection with federal loans and regulations involving the Whitewater project. But Hale was a convicted felon whose testimony could not stand by itself without the McDougals to support him.

At the outset, Starr's subordinates, mainly career federal prosecutors, never dreamed that the president could beat the rap on Whitewater. He did. This and other aspects of Clinton's activities that Starr abandoned might well have provided grounds for impeachment.

The prospect of removing any president from office is uncongenial to nearly all politicians. If there had been no referral from Starr, there surely would have been no impeachment trial at all. But once the referral came out, the House of Representatives had no choice but to impeach the president; to do otherwise would have been the last straw for the Republicans' conservative base. And with such a narrow majority after the 1998 elections, the House leadership could not afford to alienate its core supporters.

When the matter reached the Senate, the Republicans there were enormously frustrated because they found that there was no way they could move beyond Starr's extremely limited referral. Even so, an overwhelming majority of Republican senators—all but five out of fifty-five—did vote to remove Clinton from office, on just this narrow set of Lewinsky allegations. A stronger and broader referral quite likely would have had more serious consequences for the president.

•   •   •

One benefit for the Republicans that came out of the impeachment process was that the country saw that some members were not afraid to put principle ahead of popularity, and rejected the passivity and timidity of so much of the congressional leadership.

Representative Lindsey Graham, a rambunctious member of the Republican class of '94 and an impeachment manager, was always looking beyond the seamy facts to find the underlying malfeasance. As a former prosecutor, he realized that the Starr referral was insufficient. So he produced a new line of reasoning on the fact that White House aide Sidney Blumenthal, in his grand jury testimony, had inadvertently uncovered the president's obstruction of justice in describing Monica Lewinsky as a "stalker." Representing a very conservative rural district in South Carolina, Graham not only was supported by his constituents, but his performance made him a statewide figure and a rising star nationally. He is now much in demand as a speaker in congressional districts across the country.

A few of the House impeachment managers took real risks in prosecuting the case against Clinton, and none more than James Rogan. An erstwhile Democrat who had been a prosecuting attorney and judge back in California, he earned for himself the ordeal of being a target of the national Democratic party and a very tough battle for reelection in his closely divided Los Angeles–area congressional district. He showed a lot of courage in pushing for a real trial, and I think he was highly effective as a cool, dispassionate voice in the Senate proceedings, pleading the case that Clinton did commit perjury. Like Lindsey Graham, he gained instant national acclaim among rank-and-file Republicans starved for courageous heroes.

Henry Hyde, the Judiciary Committee chairman, began the impeachment as the conservative most widely admired across the political spectrum, by Democrats and journalists as well as Republicans. But he soon came under criticism (from both pro-Clinton and anti-Clinton advocates) that he did not live up to expectations.

These critics failed to recognize that in his twenty-four years in the House, Hyde had always been nonconfrontational in his tactics, even as he maintained strongly conservative positions, especially against abortion. Heading the intensely confrontational impeachment proceeding was totally out of character for him, and not a role that he at all enjoyed. Also, he was personally devastated by the revelation by the Internet magazine *Salon* of his own adultery three decades earlier, which made headlines just as the impeachment proceedings began. I give him a lot of credit for hanging in with a very tough situation.

What I found most striking about the whole process was the monolithic quality of the Democratic support for the president. This was extraordinary, and something one is not accustomed to seeing in Congress. In part this was attributable to the opinion polls, which showed the public opposed to impeachment, but there is something more here: a feeling among the congressional Democrats that Bill Clinton had saved the party just as it was going down for the third time.

Democrats in Congress were going to cut Clinton a lot of slack because of his popularity, which they saw helping them to survive. Under his leadership, the Democrats had almost won back the House in both 1996 and 1998 and were in an excellent position to do so in 2000. Near the end of the 1998 campaign, Todd Schmitz, a young lawyer who was the party's county chairman in Macomb County, Michigan (a hotly contested constituency renowned as the home of the

Reagan Democrats), told me that the Democrats owed their comeback after 1994 to Bill Clinton, and he for one would support the president until the last dog died. That was before the impeachment trial, which served to solidify this Democratic support and to make it iron hard.

But wait. Did the Democrats really owe Clinton that much? Consider the election returns of 1992 in the table shown, when Clinton was first elected president, and those of 1998, after six years of his presidency:

Partisan Division of Various Elective Offices
1992–1998

	1992			1998		
	D	**R**	**I**	**D**	**R**	**I**
U.S. House of Representatives	258	176	1	212	222	1
U.S. Senate	56	44	0	45	55	0
Governors	31	17	2	17	31	2
State Legislatures	25	8	16 split	18	17	13 split
State Legislators	4,239	3,003	17	3,881	3,469	15

D = Democrats, R = Republicans, I = Independents

The first six years of the Clinton presidency amounted to a net loss to the Democrats of 47 U.S. House members, 11 U.S. senators, 14 governors, and 358 state legislators. So

much for the gratitude of Todd Schmitz and other grass-
roots Democrats. It was a classic case of "another victory
like this, and we'll be finished." Like so much else with President Clinton, the reality is not quite what he and his spin
artists make it out to be.

• • •

Bill Clinton approached being president in a different fashion from his predecessors, and the Republicans never could
figure out how to navigate along this new political course.

The biggest change was that Clinton has run a seven-
day-a-week, twelve-month-a-year, eight-year campaign—the
"permanent campaign," Dick Morris called it. Clinton might
change his tactics, might even change his ideological direction, but the permanent campaign never changes. In *The
New Prince,* Morris's 1999 attempt to rewrite Machiavelli, he
declared, "A politician needs a permanent campaign to keep
a permanent majority. One who does not calculate how to
keep his support each day over each issue will almost inevi-
tably fail."

The first priority of the permanent campaign was to get
the president reelected in 1996 and then elect Al Gore in
2000.

The second priority was to have something in the history
books that is favorable toward Bill Clinton. The idea was
not to make the case that Clinton is a perfect person (Lord
knows that would be a thankless job), but to make sure that
he comes across as a good president. I always think of Andrew Jackson in this respect. Jackson was a murderer, a dem-
agogue, a brute, a racist, and corrupt to boot. But, venerated
by nearly two centuries of Democrats as the founder of their

party, he is considered to have been a good president. Isn't that what the history books say? Calvin Coolidge, on the other hand, was a highly moral man and highly competent public servant, but the history books tell us that he was a mediocre, if not downright bad, president. The old saw that history is written by the victors ought to be revised to say that history is written by the history professors—liberal history professors. So Clinton stands a good chance of achieving his second priority.

The third priority was to make the great American middle class dependent on government, so that ordinary citizens will attest to this credo: "I need government to get through my life." That means that government must be not just a philosophical abstraction for the elites or a safety net for the underclass, but a daily sustenance that enables ordinary people to survive and prosper—in ways that relate to the lives of the great bulk of Americans. Clinton was inspired by a 1991 article in *The American Prospect* by pollster and political consultant Stanley Greenberg (later hired for the president's 1992 campaign). Greenberg said that the Democrats should be "showing people that the state can and does serve the whole citizenry." He called the Democratic party "the party of government," which sets it apart from the Republican party, especially if middle-class Americans are encouraged to see government as an essential part of their lives.

Furthermore, Clinton really believed that government can solve all problems. He adores government in all its internal complexities, and that is a very unusual trait. Clinton is not only a politician, but a policy wonk as well. He likes to dig into details and loves to connect all kinds of policy strains to each other.

The classic case of Clinton-think was his initial justification of the bombing of Yugoslavia in March 1999, instinctively tying this military action into his pending legislative proposal for hate-crimes legislation. I was interviewing Henry Kissinger on CNN's *Crossfire* on March 23, and I shall never forget the look on the old diplomat's face when I showed him a sound bite of the president of the United States justifying his nation's bombing of Yugoslavia by comparing it to hate-crimes legislation: "That's what Kosovo's about. Look all over the world. People are still killing each other out of primitive urges because they think what is different about them is more important than what they have common." Dr. Kissinger responded somberly: "I would totally disagree with this statement. . . . It would be a very unusual use of American power." Unusual it was for the next seventy-eight days of bombing, but that was the Clinton agenda—the very essence of his presidency.

The permanent campaign led the president to adopt a particularly belligerent style of governing. He adopted the Carville Doctrine, named for his attack-dog political adviser, James Carville: You don't cross the president and not get hit back—hard—in return. Nobody attacks him without facing a fierce counterattack.

A small but telling example: the one Democratic senator who showed the slightest inclination of independence during the impeachment trial was Russell Feingold, a second-termer from Wisconsin. One of the leading voices in Congress for campaign finance reform, Feingold had won a very tough race for reelection in 1998 (against the Republican conservative insurgent from the class of '94, Representative Mark Neumann), during which he had refused to accept soft money contributions. Feingold, a lone eagle of sorts, cast some procedural votes in the impeachment trial that did not follow the party line and the Clinton lawyers' defense, though he did end up voting against the removal of Clinton from office.

A few days later after Feingold's procedural votes, President Clinton was giving a speech eulogizing Florida Governor Lawton Chiles, who had just died. He commented that Chiles "didn't go around telling you how much better he was than everybody else, because he only took $100 [as a limit on political contributions]." Although Clinton could not attack Feingold by name, Washington insiders could break the code and knew where the president was aiming.

Clinton's permanent campaign style of government exasperated the Republican leaders in Congress because they saw that it muddied the legislative process. They found Clinton extremely difficult to negotiate with, because he was all over the place—promoting one proposition, going back on another, acting as if he were in an election campaign. When they were talking to him about how to get agreement on a budget, for instance, they felt as if he were really making a campaign speech—focusing more on the voters outside, not on the people in the room.

The one time the Republicans got Clinton to accept their legislation, on welfare reform in 1996, he did so because he was on the wrong side of the polls in an election year. He knew that welfare reform polled well with this great middle class that he was trying, with considerable success, to bring back into the Democratic party. (It also had the effect of depriving Bob Dole of a campaign issue, a factor that clearly was part of Clinton's highly political decision process.)

The permanent campaign also taught Clinton that he could not succeed politically with legislative proposals as far-reaching as the 1994 health care initiative, because of the way Congress—indeed, the whole American system—works.

The Clinton health care initiative would have been passed in Japan or any European government, but because we have a different system, it is very hard to get anything done. That was the intent of the government-fearing founding fathers, and they surely succeeded.

The constitutional impediments to quick action became magnified in the contentious partisan climate of the 1990s. If a measure was very controversial, a lot of different interest groups began chipping away at it, and if your own party is not united, you cannot get it done. And let's not forget that the health care initiative failed in the Democratic 103rd Congress (the only Democratic Congress of Clinton's presidency), and not in a Republican Congress, though it was the Republicans who took the lead in defeating it. From then on, Clinton relied on bite-sized initiatives that could be market-tested in advance.

During her barnstorming train ride to the 1996 Democratic National Convention in Chicago, Hillary Rodham Clinton proposed an initiative that would mandate forty-eight hours of hospital stay for every mother of a newborn. Is that an unreasonable proposition? Hardly. But the bigger question is this: Why should the federal government be mandating hospital stays? This is something more properly handled by the health care providers, hospitals, insurance companies—or, if absolutely necessary to get government involved, the state governments. But how did the Republican Senate respond? The first week after the convention, it passed the measure on a voice vote. No profile in courage for the GOP.

Bill Clinton knew very well how hard it would be for a politician to oppose a measure like that. Being against extended maternity hospital stays is akin to being against motherhood itself. The insidious part is that Clinton was insisting that the government was going to solve this problem. Next came a federal mandate requiring employers to give time to employees to take their children to the doctor. Is that a business of the federal government? I would think not. This is an intrusion of government into employee relationships, union contracts, any number of other things. But if you ask Jan Jobholder, "Do you think your boss should be required to let you take your sick kid to the doctor?" she's going to say, definitely yes.

The president maintained, correctly, that people worry about education. But the solution he proposed was the one endorsed by the teachers' unions: smaller class size, which means hiring more teachers and requiring less work from each teacher. Parents too think it might be a good idea, providing more individual attention for their children even though there is no empirical evidence that smaller classes produce better-educated students.

Eric Hanushek, an economics professor at the University of Rochester, has done research showing that "achievement for the typical student will be unaffected by institution of the types of the class size reductions that have been recently proposed or undertaken"—other than "a dramatic increase in the costs of schooling, an increase unaccompanied by achievement gains." Other critics have alleged a negative impact because it creates an artificial shortage of teachers and encourages teachers to move from the inner city into the suburbs (where working conditions are nicer), thereby depleting the supply of experienced teachers for lower-income students.

Important in terms of the presidency's development is how everything Clinton has done has been tested by polls beforehand. Clinton's people didn't sit around thinking,

"Here's a great idea," and then put it before the citizenry. If the greatest idea in the world doesn't poll well, they won't propose it. Whether it benefits the country is irrelevant. And this reliance on polls was contagious. When Senate Majority Leader Lott began to prepare for the impeachment trial in late 1998, he met with Republican pollster Frank Luntz to find out just how people felt about the impeachment. He apparently didn't trust himself to do the right thing.

Actually, this use of polling was anything but new. The first president to use the technique was Franklin D. Roosevelt, who before Pearl Harbor surreptitiously commissioned pollster Hadley Cantril to measure how far the public would go on in sanctioning U.S. intervention in World War II. Of course, the public didn't know that the president was carrying on a correspondence with British Prime Minister Winston Churchill all this time, making the United States almost a secret co-belligerent. So although Roosevelt was anxious to find out how far he could take the public in approaching combatant status, he still knew precisely where he himself stood on the critical issue of war and peace; he merely used polling to help him develop his tactics.

The nonstop polling in the Clinton White House went far beyond anything Franklin Roosevelt could have imagined. I counted, in the 1999 State of the Union address, fifty-five new or expanded programs (other people counted even more). Almost every one of these initiatives had, in one way or another, been tested by pollsters.

It has been claimed that Clinton is not the first president to have run a quasi-campaign in the White House—that Ronald Reagan conducted a similar operation. And it is true that Reagan instituted what became a staple of the Clinton years: the issue of the day, put out by his staff and reinforced by relevant members of his administration. But while there are a lot of similarities, there are important differences. Obviously, President Reagan was very arms-length from this process, as he was arms-length from many other things. Reagan was not involved in the strategy sessions, doping things out with his communications strategist, Michael Deaver, as Bill Clinton was with Dick Morris. But there's a bigger difference. Clinton's permanent campaign strategy diminished the presidency by reducing the scope of what was under consideration.

There is a kind of a "little ball" quality to how Clinton approaches his job. "Little ball" is a baseball term, meaning you don't hit home runs; instead, you bunt, you sacrifice, you steal bases, you manufacture runs. Particularly since the defeat of the health care legislation, President Clinton has played little ball. His has not been a presidency of great ideas. I think that's why he had difficulty in selling the war in Yugoslavia to the American people, because he equated it with hate-crimes legislation instead of a credible Clinton Doctrine for the world.

Ronald Reagan did not play little ball. He played for the three-run homer. He hit some, and he struck out a lot of times. But there is no question that he put forward huge ideas. He wanted to end the Cold War with a victory and succeeded beyond all imagining. He wanted to reduce tax rates and reform the tax system; he was really more successful in that than he is given credit for because the new tax structure did not fully survive for long after he left office. He wanted to cut back the size of government and was not successful at all in that. And, in sharp contrast to Clinton, he wanted to make people less dependent on government as a force in their lives. To that end, he wanted to starve the government, by blocking its rate of growth; and here he achieved more than is generally appreciated, mainly because of his tax cuts.

Those were all big ideas. Reagan's version of John Winthrop's "shining city on a hill" was that the United States was a force for good in the world. This was somebody who devoured the publication *Human Events,* enjoyed reading *National Review,* was an inveterate clipper of newspapers, and liked big ideas and big thoughts. So I think there was quite a difference between Reagan and Clinton.

Some of President Clinton's defenders might say, "Sure, he plays little ball and is scratching out base hits and looking for the sacrifice bunt. But in the end, he reduced the size of government more than Ronald Reagan did by playing for the three-run home run. And he's had greater sustained economic growth than Reagan had. So maybe playing a scrappy type of ball isn't necessarily bad."

Leaving aside for a moment the assumptions behind this statement, I must say that the diminution of the presidency, the authority of the president as a world leader, as a national leader, is a terrible loss for our country. When the American people tell pollsters that Clinton is doing a good job, they're saying, "My life is okay. I can go out to Denny's a couple times a week and go to the movies, maybe have two cars and even a second home at the lake. But I don't trust the president; I don't believe him." Clinton spent much of his tenure with a 60 percent approval rating and a 30 percent believability rating. That cannot be good for the institution of the presidency.

As to the facts, Clinton did not reduce government more than Reagan did. What he reduced more than Reagan— much more—was the nation's military. All the figures on the reduction of government are distorted because they are so heavily biased toward the cutback in Defense Department spending. The rest of the government surely did not grow as much as many Democrats would have liked, but it certainly kept growing.

As for balancing the budget and reviving the economy, this is a debate in which I believe the Republicans have lost a lot of confidence. The argument can be made that since the 1994 election, there has been a stalemate between the parties on big ideas, except for welfare reform. This stalemate has kept the government in check and thereby improved the economic climate and permitted the economy to grow.

Clinton gets too much credit for the economic expansion of the 1990s. What the Republicans should say, which they seldom do, is that if we had a smaller government, more freedom, fewer restraints on private enterprise, and lower taxes, we would have even higher economic growth. But Clinton has deprived them of the confidence in their own ideas.

President Clinton has also undermined the Republican party by his strategy of "triangulation"—Dick Morris's concept whereby Clinton set himself up as a third force in opposition to the Republicans and his fellow Democrats. On this score, I think Morris was a sincere triangulator, whereas Clinton was not.

I know it sounds ridiculous to call Dick Morris sincere and Bill Clinton deceptive, but I don't think President Clinton really ever believed in a third force. Rather, he believed in big government. That he is ideologically closer to Stan Greenberg than Dick Morris is clear from his laundry list of government programs in the 1999 State of the Union address. He just does what he can and no longer attempts the unattainable. But his tactics have drawn many Republicans into a kind of reverse triangulation, where they say, "Man, we don't want to be left out here alone. We want to say yes, we're for more teachers too. We want more money for these things, but we'll put the money in the states instead of the federal government." That's a triangulation of a kind. I think he sucked the Republicans into a triangulation even while not being very triangular himself. Thus, by pretending to move to the center, he drew the Republicans away from their own beliefs and toward the Democrats' view of the world. In this way, Bill Clinton has remade the Republican party in his own image.

• • •

There is no question about Bill Clinton's being a very polarizing person, in a way that goes far beyond the usual partisan rivalries. For example, I don't think the Republicans ever really hated Jimmy Carter. They had contempt for him and didn't think he was a good president, but they didn't burn with hatred the way they came to about Clinton.

I think that Bill Clinton was looked upon by many Republicans as embodying everything wrong with America in the 1990s: someone who didn't serve his country, who is a philanderer, who was apparently a counterculture person in his youth and used illegal substances but came to say, "I didn't inhale." In the eyes of many Republicans, he gets away with everything.

Clinton's campaign mantra incessantly stressed playing by the rules, but he clearly did not play by the rules himself. People didn't understand Whitewater, but they think he was involved in some sharp dealing back in Arkansas—and got away with it. His wife did questionable investing in cattle futures—and got away with it. He helped finance the 1996 campaign by dealing with shady characters like John Huang and Johnny Chung—and got away with it. A lot of middle-income or lower-middle-income Republicans, who live solid lives, deeply resented what they perceive to be Bill Clinton's cavalier attitude toward his own responsibility. And this led to a lot of hatred.

Even mainstream Republicans who voted for him in 1992 lost their trust in him and came to see him as an extremely slippery character. I think many business people regarded this administration as much less business friendly than it pretended to be, especially at the regulatory level. Industrialists found themselves oppressed by tougher safety and environmental rules. Bankers saw the federal government seeking to force them out of business in granting student loans and home mortgages.

One of the most disturbing things about Bill Clinton, as a president, is that he remains connected with his twenty-two-year-old self in a way that other politicians are not. He seems unaware that people expected him to live up to his promises about his own personal behavior.

I think that a crossroads was reached with his *60 Minutes* interview in January 1992, in which he answered allegations by a former cabaret singer named Gennifer Flowers that she had engaged in a torrid twelve-year adulterous affair with him. "That allegation is false," said Clinton, battling for the Democratic presidential nomination. But he also admitted marital "problems," then asked whether it were true that "if people have problems in their marriage and there are things in the past which they don't want to discuss which are painful to them, that they can't run?" The meaning was unmistakable: infidelity in the past, yes; but no more messing around.

If the president had behaved himself after that interview with no more messing around—no Monica Lewinsky, no Kathleen Willey, no more slipperiness with the truth—I do not think we would be seeing such hatred of him. Sure, there were Clinton haters before all the allegations about Monica Lewinsky came out, but the sex scandals definitely fed into the existing hostility to him. People who tended to vote Republican were angry that he had not closed the book on his twenty-two-year-old self. Their attitude was that the rest of us have grown up, so why can't he?

Also feeding the animosity was the first lady, perhaps an even more polarizing figure than her husband. While a heroine to many women (and a martyr after the Monica Lewinsky affair, which made her a Senate candidate), she frightened others. Beyond the fact that she is an even stronger believer in big government and more of a liberal than the president, there is a hardness about Hillary Rodham Clinton that frightens conservatives.

Is this just a manifestation of Republican chauvinists who are afraid of strong women? (The first lady kept her maiden name in the early years of their marriage and then restored the "Rodham" as her middle name once her husband was elected president.) Assuredly, there was much of that. Nevertheless, Mrs. Clinton's hauteur disturbed not only traditional women but people with more progressive views.

As a practicing lawyer in Little Rock while supposedly the first lady of Arkansas, she developed her own agenda of liberal causes (most notably children's rights) much as her idol, Eleanor Roosevelt, had done in the White House. Her contempt toward those who chose to live their lives differently was revealed by her comment in the spring of 1992 that "I suppose I could have stayed home, baked cookies, and had teas" but that she "decided . . . to fulfill my profession." The outcry after that outburst put her on the shelf for the balance of what was then the most important year in her husband's life. She emerged after the election as the manager of the president's ill-fated health care proposal: authoritarian, secretive, arrogant. After the program crashed and burned, leading to the 1994 electoral disaster, the first lady's profile was lowered radically. Not until her image was transformed to that of the wronged woman did she return to the spotlight as a candidate for the U.S. Senate from New York, a state with which she had no previous connection. Once she reappeared in this new mode, hostility toward her rose again.

President Clinton's permanent campaign style of government also threw management of public business off-kilter. In earlier administrations, presidents met often with the cabinet as a team, as a senior board of policy advisers, but Clinton did not. Through the first two and three-quarters years of his second term, he conducted only two cabinet meetings—one to deny the Lewinsky affair (and to embarrass the cabinet members who avowed their belief in his lie), the other to say that he had lied a year earlier. Clinton preferred to rely almost exclusively on himself, exhibiting enormous self-confidence about politics and policy.

Moreover, the stature of White House staff members declined sharply. Instead of big business executives or former congressmen, Clinton's top advisers in his second term tended to be people who had made their living by working on campaigns. They were quite clever, but not people with lofty reputations. This was a sharp contrast to Clinton's first-term staff, which more closely followed the tradition of formidable personages serving the president.

Consider the Clinton-created cabinet-level post of National Economic Council director, for example. The first person to hold the job was a multimillionaire investment banker, Robert E. Rubin, the former co-chairman of Goldman Sachs. When Rubin became secretary of the treasury in 1995, he was replaced by Gene Sperling, a talented young man, but one who had hitherto always been somebody's staff person. (He had been an aide to New York Governor Mario Cuomo before joining the 1992 Clinton campaign as a mid-level aide.)

Or consider that the man who ended up as Clinton's White House chief of staff after the 1998 election was John Podesta, who also had previously been a political operative. Podesta was not a powerful figure in his own right, in the mold of his prestigious predecessors Erskine Bowles (a North Carolina industrialist) and Leon Panetta (a former chairman of the House Budget Committee) or, in the Bush administration, John Sununu (a former governor of New Hampshire). The first White House chief of staff in today's mode was President Eisenhower's: Sherman Adams, another former governor of New Hampshire and a truly formidable figure. In the Clinton White House, by contrast, political mechanics abounded.

In terms of partisan combat, Clinton's relentless focus on maintaining his poll numbers has reinforced a tendency among the Republicans to pursue what they considered the best thing pragmatically rather than the right thing to do. They have tended to abandon legislation or issues that are controversial or difficult, even if they are desirable. They have pulled away from term limits, from school choice, from opposing racial quotas, from the elimination of goverment departments, from radical deregulation. They have even pulled away from truly radical tax reduction, historically the Republicans' best issue.

A particularly telling example of what has happened to the Republicans occurred on April 15, 1999. The conservative group Americans for Tax Reform had planned a rally on the Capitol steps to mark the day that income taxes are due. One of the highlights of the rally was to be the presentation of "Friends of the American Taxpayer" awards to several members of Congress, and the idea was that the entire Republican leadership would be there. House Speaker Dennis Hastert did turn up, but Senate Majority Leader Trent Lott did not. Lott said that the rally conflicted with a Republican leadership meeting on the budget. But in reality, one event was scheduled for 1:30, the other for 3:15, so Lott could have attended both if he had wanted to.

What actually was going on was that Lott did not want to put the emphasis on taxes that day; he wanted to emphasize the budget. The reason: Clinton could use the tax issue to slam the GOP—"tax cuts for the rich"—whereas the budget is a complicated document that Congress assembles itself, with no presidential input if the legislative branch so desires. Lott wanted to emphasize what he was doing as Senate leader and not tackle a big controversial issue. That is a Clinton effect too: to do what is easier to accomplish within your ideological framework.

The problem for the Republicans is that in mimicking Clinton—doing what is easier, as opposed to what is more important—they have tossed away much of what they believe in. Having seen how damaged Clinton became after the health care fiasco in 1994, the Republicans, with a lot to lose after becoming the majority party in Congress, have become increasingly risk averse.

That leads to the critical question for the 2000 elections: if the Republican party is not going to deal with term limits, abortion, affirmative action, reduction of government, tax credits, tax reform, or deregulation, then does it make that much difference who is in power? The Republicans have to make the case that it does, and the only way to do so is to have the courage of their convictions.

That courage is less and less likely to come from the Republican party in Congress, which has been intimidated by Clinton and the pressures of Washington political life in general. Republican members of Congress worry about something that governors don't worry about and that the rank-and-file Republicans certainly don't worry about: making the trains run on time.

What terrifies them most of all, in keeping with the railroad metaphor, is a "train wreck"—a worst-case legislative scenario, usually thought of as another government shutdown, as in 1995–1996. The next worst scenario is that the government doesn't close, but that a logjam at the end of the session gives the president all of the bargaining power over the budget (because he can threaten to veto the whole thing), forcing the Republicans to accept things that they shouldn't accept, as indeed they did in 1998.

But the hard truth is that a train wreck, this horrible calamity that the congressional Republicans fear so much, is something that concerns only people in Washington. People outside the Beltway couldn't give a damn about the budget negotiations; they care more about their tax bill, their neighborhoods, their retirement.

And that is why Trent Lott made a foolish error—small

but symbolic—in not going to the anti-tax rally on the Capitol steps. He missed an opportunity to position himself and his party on a controversial, important question. He focused on the budget resolution so that he could avoid a train wreck. That is a real Washington mind-set. The hard reality is that nobody ever has gotten elected or defeated because of a train wreck. Even the government shutdown in 1995 was really more about power politics and who had the upper hand in Washington than it was with the electorate. But it had a long-lasting, corrosive effect on Republicans. Call it loss of courage.

• • •

The picture of Republicans' remaking themselves in the image of William Jefferson Clinton is not very attractive. Why should voters want Clintonized Republicans when they can vote for the real thing?

But I believe there is a winning platform for the Grand Old Party, based on principle rather than Clinton-like strategizing. It will take courage and also skill. Some of its planks are obvious: tax reduction, tax reform, and Social Security reform. Others are more difficult from the standpoint of keeping together the Republican constituency, much less winning over a national majority: steadfastness on opposing abortion; reaching out to African Americans, Hispanics, and women while abjuring racial quotas; supporting global free trade but adhering to a nationalism that avoids unwarranted intervention in disputes not connected to the national security; accepting and welcoming religious conservatives. Still more difficult, the party should embrace two important reforms that have been universally abhorred by the party leadership, one cryptically and the other openly: term limits and campaign finance reform.

To the Clintonized Republican leadership, this course may look suicidal. In fact, all they need to do is remember what they stand for and then stand by it.

PART TWO

Ten Things Republicans Can Do to Win in 2000

Use the Budget Surplus to Cut Taxes— for Everyone

I have said many times that God put the Republicans on earth to cut taxes. If they don't cut taxes, they have no overriding rationale for existence.

People hate to pay taxes. The young people I talk to are appalled when they get their first paycheck and see how much has been taken out of it. Older people are no happier about the government's bite either. Every time a candidate talks about taxes, he does well. *No seeker of public office has ever been hurt by calling for tax cuts.*

Liberals are quick to point out to people like me that surveys consistently show that tax cuts are a low priority among likely voters, who tell pollsters that they consider education, saving Social Security, and even such an abstruse goal as drawing down the national debt as more important priorities for the government to address.

But there is a problem with the polls. Tax cuts come out fifth or sixth in priority on voters' lists because people don't want to admit that they would rather have money come back to them as tax cuts than to be spent on such conventionally worthy causes as education or debt reduction. It's a matter of being embarrassed to answer the pollster's questions honestly.

Even so, there are a lot of younger politicians in the Republican party who are eager to bring the tax issue to the fore. In the 1998 midterm election (not a very good election for Republicans, certainly), two candidates particularly stood out on this issue.

In Janesville, Wisconsin, a twenty-eight-year-old career political activist named Paul Ryan ran for the seat once held by a prominent Democrat: the late Les Aspin, the Clinton administration's first secretary of defense. Aspin had been followed in the House by Mark Neumann, the self-made millionaire home builder who had run afoul of the Appropriations Committee leadership and was running for the Senate against the Democratic incumbent, Russell Feingold.

Neumann had put the ephemeral goal of debt reduction ahead of tax cuts. In contrast, Ryan was a supply-sider who had been a staffer and speechwriter at the Empower America organization (put together by Bill Bennett and Jack Kemp), and he was a protegé of Vin Weber, the former congressman from Minnesota, a prominent Republican insider and conservative supply-sider. With Neumann at the top of the ticket as the Republican candidate for the U.S. Senate, Ryan had to balance lip-service to Neumann's position with his own emphasis on reducing taxes. It worked. Ryan won his congressional race in that closely contested district, while Neumann lost for the Senate.

In Allentown, Pennsylvania, thirty-seven-year-old Pat Toomey ran for an open seat in a predominantly working-class Democratic district. The seat previously was held by Paul McHale, a three-term Democrat who chose not to run for reelection in 1998 and became notorious in his final months in office by first calling for President Clinton's resignation and then voting for his impeachment.

Toomey had spent his whole career in the private sector (as an investment banker, international financial consultant, and founder and operator of a restaurant business) and was a virtual unknown in local politics. He campaigned on repealing the Internal Revenue Code and replacing it with a flat tax. All the polls indicated that that was the wrong thing to do, but people loved it. It was supposed to be a toss-up race, but he was the upset winner in a six-way Republican primary and, in a bad Republican year, he won handsomely in the general election with 55 percent of the vote.

•   •   •

The issue of tax cuts became more relevant than ever in 1999 because of the budget surplus. Ten years earlier, all we heard about from Democrats and "deficit hawks" was the ominous specter of "deficits as far as the eye can see"—a phrase originated by President Reagan's unfaithful budget director, David Stockman.

This is a classic example of the problems of straight-line projections, when one projects what is happening now into the future at the same rate. What the doomsayers did not count on were the underlying growth patterns in the U.S. economy and the relative moderation in the growth of government spending that followed the Republican takeover of Congress in 1994. During those five years, with the exception of welfare reform, very few major bills—good or bad— were passed into law.

With less spending and less government interference, the economy was able to grow at a slow but steady rate, to produce the unexpected surplus. President Clinton claimed that the 1993 tax increase balanced the budget, but the figures just don't add up. Had the extra revenue been accompanied by ascending levels of government spending, the deficit would have persisted. While one cannot accurately project the precise rate of economic growth had Democratic control of Congress continued, it is clear that the grandiose Clinton projects (headed by health care reform) surely would have slowed growth. And what is truly indisputable is that the 1993 tax bill has resulted in the highest level of taxation in dollars per capita since World War II—higher than during World War I, higher than during the Korean War, higher than during the Vietnam War, and higher than during the entire course of the Cold War.

This question was raised in 1999: What to do with the surplus? There are realistically only two options: spend it or give it back in taxes. The idea that the money is going to sit around and reduce the national debt is unlikely in the extreme. If it is out there and not given back in taxes, it is definitely going to be spent.

The Republicans, however, were frightened—often terrified, actually—by the Democrats, who say, "Don't spend the surplus; save it for Social Security" (whatever that means—not much, as I'll discuss later). So, they have said, "Okay, we won't send it back in taxes, we'll put it in a lockbox, so it won't be touched." My skepticism about this procedure is overwhelming. If the money is not restored to the taxpayer, it will be spent because the propensity of Congress is to spend even when it doesn't have the money; when it does have the money, that propensity is magnified many times.

The first bill going through the Republican-controlled Senate in 1999, the military pay bill, established new entitlements for servicemen and veterans far out into the future, which of course cut into the surplus. No lockbox can withstand the assault of a Congress ready to spend if there is no tax cut to put the money out of their reach. The Republicans pinned their hopes on this lockbox idea, and trotted out all sorts of focus groups and polls showing that it's a good idea. In the real world, the question of whether we would just have more spending increases if there were no tax cuts was partially answered when spending for the war in Yugoslavia immediately began reducing the surplus in the spring of 1999.

Of course, the foes of tax cuts soon made clear that the tax receipts not reserved for the lockbox also had to be dedicated to reducing debt, thereby expanding the pool of funds for "investments"—that is, government spending. It's clear enough. Revenues not returned to the taxpayer surely will be spent.

• • •

The only lockbox that was working was the box that the Republicans have constructed for themselves on the issue of tax cuts. The problem goes back almost half a century. In 1953, Dwight D. Eisenhower, the first Republican president in twenty years, took office along with a Republican Congress. This was the first time since 1929–1930 that the presidency, the Senate, and the House were all controlled by Republicans—and the last time for the next forty-six years, going into the 2000 elections.

The first action by the newly installed chairman of the Ways and Means Committee, Dan Reed, a crusty old conservative from upstate New York, was to pass a big tax cut—drafting it in his committee even before the new Republican president was inaugurated. The people around Eisenhower were so alarmed that this was a budget buster that after Ways and Means approved the bill they got the House Rules Committee to block the tax cut from getting onto the floor. And so Eisenhower never had a really serious across-the-board tax cut, even though he had three budget surpluses in eight years, which is not bad. But he also had three recessions and lost his majority in Congress in 1954—never to be regained during his two full terms in office. The Democrats were high in the saddle by the time he left, following their congressional landslide in the recession year of 1958 and the victory of John F. Kennedy in 1960.

In 1968, Richard Nixon campaigned for president against the surtax imposed by President Lyndon Johnson to enable him to finance simultaneously the War on Poverty and the war in Vietnam. But once in office, Nixon listened to his advisers, who told him that repealing the surtax was a budget buster, and so he retained it in violation of his campaign promise, balanced the budget, and had stagflation for the rest of his tenure in office, guaranteeing solid Democratic control of Congress throughout his presidency. That made Nixon the first elected president never to enjoy control of either house by his own party. (The second was George Bush.)

Succeeding the disgraced Nixon, Gerald Ford inherited a failing economy and prescribed austerity, rejecting the notion of tax reduction. George Bush as president also dreaded busting the budget and famously broke his word and increased taxes in 1990, leading to his defeat by Bill Clinton two years later.

The only really successful Republican president in the postwar era was Ronald Reagan, who instead of following the Eisenhower and Nixon models, stuck to his guns. Combining the classical economics he had learned as an undergraduate at little Eureka College in Illinois with the supply-side ideology pressed on him by Congressman Jack Kemp, he became the first Republican since Calvin Coolidge to engage seriously in tax cutting. It made Reagan a very popular president, who presided over general prosperity except for the recession of 1982–1983 (which was itself caused by the Federal Reserve's effective but painful tight-money policy to combat inflation and by the delay in the full effect of the 25 percent across-the-board tax cut).

Ever since Reagan left office, however, the tax system has become steadily, though unobtrusively, more progressive. This has come about in part by increasing taxation in the upper brackets (as with Clinton's 1993 tax bill), but mainly by excluding taxes for the lower brackets and providing rebates for low-income workers. The earned-income tax credit, instituted during the Reagan administration to help the working poor, became a new welfare scheme. The chart on page 90 shows the distribution of the tax burden over the past twenty years.

As we can see, fewer and fewer income taxes are paid by people at the low end of the salary scale and more and more by those at the upper reaches. So in a distribution table on any kind of across-the-board income tax cut, the small percentage of people earning more than $100,000—that is, the top 4.8 percent of taxpayers—get most of the benefits. Of course, they pay most of the taxes. That's the dirty little secret, and that's the Republicans' major problem. (A second problem is that more than 70 percent of Americans pay more in payroll taxes for Social Security and Medicare than they do in income taxes; I'll address this later on.)

Whenever the Republicans propose an across-the-board tax cut, they get hammered for promoting "tax cuts for the

Percentage of Federal Tax Revenues Paid
by Different Income Groups
1975–1995

Income Level	1975	1985	1995
Over $100,000	9.7%	23.7%	47.6%
$75,000–$100,000		6.7%	11.6%
$50,000–$75,000	10.7%*	17.2%	17.0%
$25,000–$50,000	23.8%	35.1%	17.8%
Under $25,000	55.9%	17.2%	6.1%

Source: Internal Revenue Service.

*The IRS does not have separate data for $50,000–$75,000 and $75,000–$100,000 in 1975. The 10.7 percent covers $50,000–$100,000.

rich." That's why Bob Dole's presidential campaign proposal for a 15 percent tax cut died in 1996 (leaving aside the fact that he never truly believed in it), and that's why similar proposals have gotten nowhere in five years of GOP control in Congress—not even the much ballyhooed 1999 Republican tax cut. The Republicans know that tax cuts are a winning issue, but they haven't figured out how to frame it. It's all the more difficult because the Democrats are inexorable in trying to steepen the progressivity of the tax system, with President Clinton in 1999 unveiling a "savings" plan that would further reduce what little income taxes are paid by the lowest income earners.

With the Republican grass roots desperately disappointed by the GOP performance over four and one-half years in the majority, and with the 2000 election in the offing, Congress in midsummer 1999 moved toward passage of what in terms of estimated revenue loss would be the largest tax reduction since the Reagan cuts of 1981—destined for a sure Clinton veto.

Had the Republicans really learned their lesson and screwed up their courage? Not quite. Speaker Dennis Hastert had to plead with recalcitrant Republicans to pass a tax bill in the House. The most generous version amounted to a tax reduction of only 25 cents for every dollar of surplus. While the estimated ten-year revenue of $782 billion seemed audacious, it was modest in terms of the $3 trillion-plus surplus. But that price tag was deceptive. The final version of the bill was so packed with special interest provisions won by Republican lobbyists and the marriage penalty relief demanded by the Christian conservatives that a modest 10 percent across-the-board tax cut was reduced to a paltry 1 percent. So backloaded were the tax cuts in the ten-year bill that a computer study by Stephen Moore of the Cato Institute showed that the total reduction in the level of federal taxation would be 0.6 percent in the first year, 0.8 percent in the second year, and 1.4 percent in the third year.

This caution was intensified by a new desire to use the surplus to reduce the debt—in the expectation, certainly not borne out by economic history, that debt reduction would necessarily bring down interest rates (which actually are much more affected by the Federal Reserve's money-market operations). Unlikely though debt reduction might be, the idea had infected Republican thinking.

To cajole enough House Republicans to pass the bill, Speaker Hastert had to agree to make tax cuts conditional on anticipated debt reduction. Thus, considering the subsequent lowering of tax cuts, the probable revenue loss for the bill was much closer to $500 billion than $800 billion. Put it this way: If the Federal Reserve were to increase interest rates to combat inflation, the anticipated debt reduction would be greatly reduced, and might possibly vanish—and there goes any tax cut.

Not for the first time, Jack Kemp was a voice in the wilderness. He asked: "Would we trade all the investment in high technology since the early '80s, made possible by the Reagan tax cuts and the 1997 capital gains reduction, for slightly lower federal interest payments?" He added that "no reduction of an already shrinking national debt ever produced prosperity."

At the same time, the Democrats have figured out their own general solution: targeted tax cuts. President Clinton has had a lot of success in promoting tuition tax credits, per-child tax breaks, tax advantages for investments in poor neighborhoods, and, indeed, for nearly every other imaginable good cause. Clinton's pollsters market-test the ideas before he proposes them, and it's hard for the Republicans to stand in opposition to promoting such worthy activities.

But the more I've learned about targeted tax cuts, the more I realize that their implications for all Americans—not just Republicans—are not so wonderful. I recall when the light went on in my head, during a 1996 CNN interview with Tom Daschle, the Democratic Senate minority leader. He was pushing Clinton's college tuition tax credit (later passed by the Republican-controlled Congress), and I said, "If I would rather buy a Corvette than send my kids to college or I don't have any kids, then I don't get the tax credit?" I thought Daschle would die; he didn't know whether to laugh or take me seriously. He said, "You might want to buy a Corvette, but I don't think the government ought to help you do that."

Now this is a philosophical point. Is it "helping" you do something if you are overcharged on taxes and just getting your own money back? And since it's your own money, why shouldn't you spend it on something you want to buy? I used the Corvette example because I drive a Corvette. But beyond that, it is really an impractical car—it's expensive, gas-guzzling, no luggage space, only two passenger seats, uncomfortable, and a bumpy ride. But what if you want to buy it? I did in 1961 when I was a $10,000-a-year reporter for *The Wall Street Journal* and paid $5,000 for a brand-new blue Corvette.

A ridiculous decision, but that's the lost element of the American equation—freedom. President Clinton never used that little word in his seventy-seven-minute State of the Union address in 1999, and the Republicans don't use it often either. It's very hard for a Republican politician to say that you have a right to get a tax cut to buy a Corvette.

The day after the State of the Union, the president went to a pep rally in the big hockey arena in Buffalo, New York. The crowd was roaring, and the president deviated from the poll-tested ideas and rhetoric to say what was really on his mind about what should be done with the surplus: "We could give it all back to you and hope you spend it right. But I think here's the problem." There could be Social Security bankruptcy "if you don't spend it right." Then Clinton went further by suggesting that people might say, "Mr. President, give me the money. I'd rather have a new car." But that, he suggested, would be wrong. (Yes, he really said that, ad-libbed it and never said it again, considering the sensibilities of the United Auto Workers, but that is the real, unpurified Clinton.)

So this is a freedom issue, which I think is a very good issue for the Republicans: the ability for people to use their own money as they choose. The pollster John Zogby, at my request, asked Americans on February 15–17, 1999, whether people, recognizing they "have responsibilities to the nation as a whole" would rather spend the money from a tax cut "for good purposes defined by the federal government" or, alternatively, "be free to spend it as you wish." The "spend it as you wish" option won, 68.1 percent to 21.7 percent; it fared even better among African Americans (73.1 percent), women (71.2 percent), young people (73.1 percent), independents (70.1 percent), and women working outside the home (75.1 percent). This is a good issue for the GOP if the party wants to use it.

By the time of the 1998 election, targeted tax cuts had become the staple of left-wing Democrats who no longer could sell straight government spending programs. Representative Rosa DeLauro of Connecticut, doyenne of the congressional hard left, insisted that tax cuts be limited strictly to finance "health care, school modernization, child care [and] stay-at-home parents." These are commendable goals, but the issue of freedom is raised by the government's dictating that the money it has overcharged its citizens can be returned to them only if they spend it for carefully mandated purposes.

The Republicans have been so intimidated by targeted tax cuts that some of them have even come up with their own targeted tax plans. The Republicans started down this road in 1997 with the Children's Tax Credit, pushed by the Christian Coalition. They also made a great push for the repeal of the marriage penalty, which is, in effect, a targeted tax cut (also backed by the Christian Coalition). Representative Nancy Johnson of Connecticut, a Republican representing a liberal district and suffering from having voted to impeach the president in 1998, proposed her own targeted tax program promoting health care, child care, education, affordable housing, urban revitalization, and preservation of open space, as well as an end to the marriage penalty. The message: spend the money as we say and you get a tax cut. With support from as few as five other Republicans, she and the Democrats could pass it in the House.

Ted Stevens of Alaska, the prototypical "old bull" chairman of the Senate Appropriations Committee and surely no Nancy Johnson–style moderate, has also come out in favor of targeted tax cuts. I asked Stevens whether a test of how the Republican party does its job would be whether it passes an across-the-board tax reduction. He replied: "No. No, I don't really favor across-the-board. I favor targeted tax reductions, and I believe we should make some. I've got a child about ready to go to college, you know. I've put five kids through school before. The cost of sending one in there, now, is about the same as sending five before. The middle-income and lower-income people need more money of their own to spend, and I think we have to have some targeted tax reductions."

Ted Stevens, meet Rosa DeLauro.

What's going on here is that many Republicans have been frightened away from broad-based tax relief and have bought into the Democrats' vision of social engineering disguised as targeted tax cuts, which are often very small. But although it seems unpopular right now to oppose targeted tax cuts, I do believe that if the Republicans can reframe the issue as a question of freedom and say that it's your money to do with as you want, rather than the government's money to spend on approved social purposes, they can make it a cornerstone of a winning campaign. They appeared to have made a modest start toward that goal in the summer of 1999 with a very long way to go, but stumbled badly when they ended up with that ludicrous 1 percent across-the-board tax cut and then gave up the fight for the year.

Endorse a National Sales Tax to Replace the Internal Revenue Code

Tax cuts are only the first step if the Republicans are to have a real impact on how the public's business is done. After all, today's tax cut can be reversed by tomorrow's tax increase. What is needed, and what has been sorely lacking from Republican leaders, is a realistic plan for overhauling the entire federal tax structure. As we've seen, across-the-board tax cuts have a tough time flying politically, because of the distributional effects, so the Republicans need to line up behind a plan that would change the whole system radically.

They had a splendid opportunity in 1995, right after they won control of Congress. During that year, I traveled with some Republicans in their districts, and at town hall meetings they always asked the audience, "Do you want to keep the present tax system as it is?" Never did more than one or two hands go up. In Michigan someone did raise his hand, and Congressman Dick Chrysler said, "Oh, that guy's an accountant." But the Republicans never got behind one single plan, and that gave the Democrats time to cast them as favoring "tax cuts for the rich." The Republicans have been so frightened by the Democratic attack that they have walked away from the solution to their problem and began wringing their hands.

I can't help but contrast this state of affairs to twenty years ago. The Republican party was not doing well. Jimmy Carter had been elected president in 1976, Watergate was still fresh in voters' minds, and there were big Democratic majorities in Congress. Though in hindsight we think of Ronald Reagan as the unquestioned leader of the Republican party at this time, a president-in-waiting, that was by no means a widely shared opinion among the GOP rank and file. Not for the first or last time, the party was leaderless—just drifting.

Then, in 1978, the Republican National Committee did a very interesting thing. Under the chairmanship of a former senator from Tennessee named William Brock (not considered a staunch conservative by any means), who was desperate to pump some life into the party, the Republican National Committee took a policy position: it endorsed the Kemp-Roth bill, which called for a 30 percent across-the-board tax cut (inspired by the supply-side guru Jude Wanniski, then an editorial writer for *The Wall Street Journal*).

There are very few precedents of the national committee of either major party doing anything like that, but Brock felt he had to do something. GOP leadership on the Hill was not merely unimpressive but politically moribund. Although the Kemp-Roth endorsement did not result in big gains in the 1978 midterm elections, it did give the party something to build on for the 1980 presidential election, especially after Ronald Reagan embraced Kemp-Roth (partly to forestall Jack Kemp from entering the presidential race and splitting the conservative vote).

Today, however, there is no Kemp-Roth. Competing plans abound, but there is no party position, no solution put forward. Although people are upset and hate the current tax code, Republicans have not said, "Here is our alternative," and laid it out for the public to judge, as they did in 1978 and 1980, when they said, "Here is our alternative, and it's Kemp-Roth."

•   •   •

The only viable alternatives to the current tax code are a flat tax and a national sales tax. From what I've seen, people love the idea of a flat tax, of writing the tax on a postcard, of the rich not having loopholes. A true flat tax of 17 percent, with no exemptions, would come close to replacing the revenue of the current income tax, and House Majority Leader Dick Armey became its most visible proponent in the new Republican Congress in 1995.

But a funny thing happened on the way to the flat tax: the Republican leadership in Congress couldn't pull the trigger. House Speaker Newt Gingrich enthusiastically embraced the flat tax, with two little caveats: two big tax exemptions, for home mortgage payments and for charitable contributions, must remain. Armey argued strenuously against Gingrich's position. "It's imperative," he said. "Every flat tax effort in the past came unraveled when somebody decided, 'I got room for compromise.' Or 'I can make this exception.'"

Sure enough, the unraveling began immediately. The Republican governors of the states with big income taxes (led by California and New York) insisted on maintaining the deductibility of state income taxes. There was little resistance from Capitol Hill. Then the religious conservatives insisted on including the "pro-family" $500-per-child tax credit that had been part of the Contract with America.

And there was a darker side to what was happening.

Nobel laureate economist Milton Friedman, in his mordant style, dismissed all the talk about scrapping the Internal Revenue Code by noting that the lobbyist community of Washington had a vested interest in complexity. No more bitter foes of tax simplicity could be found than these lobbyists, boasting a symbiotic relationship with members of Congress in both parties who relied on them for campaign contributions (a subject I will soon address at greater length).

Then came Malcolm S. Forbes, Jr.

Unintentionally Steve Forbes was the worst thing to happen to the flat tax. He came out of nowhere in 1996 to mount a serious challenge to Bob Dole for the Republican presidential nomination. The multimillionaire magazine publisher had never run for anything and was not a very exciting speaker. (His father, Malcolm S. Forbes, Sr., was an experienced politician who had run unsuccessfully for governor of New Jersey in the 1950s and was a fabulous, party-giving character. He was very exciting; his son is not.) But Steve Forbes latched onto something that he had been pushing in *Forbes* magazine and his column for years: the flat tax. In so doing, with plentiful television advertising financed out of his own fortune, he pounded the hell out of Dole—out of all of the establishment candidates, in fact—for being taxers, and the next thing you knew, Forbes was rising in the polls. He was running first in New Hampshire at one point.

The other candidates and the party establishment had to counterattack, and they had to kill not only Forbes but the flat tax as well. Lamar Alexander, Phil Gramm, Bob Dole, even Pat Buchanan, were all pounding on the flat tax as a plaything of the idle rich. Dick Armey made a great remark at that time: "I understand why they had to kill the messenger, but why did they have to kill the message, too?" Politically the flat tax never quite recovered from the battering it took from the leaders of the Republican party in 1996.

What's worst of all is that the main criticisms of the flat tax fed one another in a vicious circle. First, the critics focused on the exemptions that the flat tax would eliminate, especially the home mortgage deduction, and then they claimed that it was too sweet a deal for the rich. But if you keep the home mortgage and charitable deductions (and a few others), you then have to raise the rate to 26 or 28 percent. Then the flat tax for lower-income people gets to be too high—higher than what they are paying now, but still lower than the current rate the rich are paying. So to make it fairer to ordinary people, you have to have two rates, or even three. And then you have the idea that this is an unfinished book. If you come back the next year, there will be new proposals for new deductions for worthy constituencies. The next thing you know, you'll have reconstituted the Internal Revenue Code as it exists today. Milton Friedman had it right.

• • •

A national sales tax is an even more radical proposal than the flat tax, but potentially it has more going for it. It takes the simplicity argument of the flat tax one step further, as was shown when Dick Armey and Billy Tauzin, a congressman from Louisiana (and former Democratic regional whip who had crossed the aisle to become a Republican only three months before the GOP takeover in the 1994 elections), began a nationwide series of debates in a "Scrap the Code" forum in Mobile, Alabama. Armey displayed a billboard-sized facsimile of the ten-line income tax form his flat tax system would use, listing wages and salaries, a standard deduction to be subtracted, and a single tax rate to be applied to all income above the deduction. That's all. No attached annexes. No complicated computations. No accountants.

Tauzin then displayed his poster, the same size as Armey's but perfectly blank. "Here's the one you need to send in with my plan," he drawled. Nothing. People would not even have to keep track of their earnings. Under one version, the income tax would be abolished and replaced by a levy on all retail transactions, with no exemptions—none on food, medical services and home purchases. All taxpayers would receive a rebate (the functional equivalent of Armey's standard deduction, which eliminated income taxes for lower-income Americans) that would help the poor much more than the rich.

In order for a sales tax to be "revenue neutral"—that is, to replace all the revenue collected by the current system—the rate will have to be very high, in the neighborhood of 23 percent (not counting as much as 5 percent for state tax). This is where the Republicans need true fortitude, because people will gasp and say, "One-quarter of a dollar on everything! That's too much. And it's not fair! Why should a guy flipping hamburgers have to pay 25 percent of his income, while a millionaire does the same thing?" What they don't take into account, however, is that the millionaire is going to buy different things than the guy flipping hamburgers, and the rebate—a fixed amount for all taxpayers based on the cost of essentials—will restore the progressivity. If the annual rebate is, say, $2,000, a person making $25,000 a year may find it very comfortable, whereas for a person making $4 million it's meaningless. Also, if the regressive payroll tax is eliminated, as it should be, the working person is helped

(though the myth of Social Security as an insurance system is ended.)

I believe that if the ordinary working person, the person working on a production line or a fast-food restaurant, is given the choice of a clean paycheck with no deductions plus paying this whopping sales tax, or the existing system, that person would take the sales tax. (That means neither income tax nor payroll tax, no tax on interest, dividends on capital gains, no estate tax.)

Of course, the Republicans have to be willing to talk it up and explain it. And one other thing is absolutely necessary to make a sales tax work: the income tax and the Sixteenth Amendment (which authorized the income tax) must be repealed, so that Congress can never restore the income tax. The worst of all scenarios would be a sales tax coupled with the existing income tax system, which is what Europe uses and which has been a constant drag on the continental economy.

This obviously is going to take some time and some creative thinking. Republican Congressman Christopher Cox of California has proposed a phasing in of the sales tax, or a delay of the sales tax and an interim period under a flat tax. That may be a very salubrious outcome, but to achieve it will be difficult and require real leadership. This is an area where the presidential candidate of the Republican party, not being part of the Washington congressional establishment, can take the initiative and make an impact.

Or we can have four more years of tinkering and dithering.

Establish True Personal Accounts for Social Security

President Clinton and the Democrats view Social Security as one issue where they hold all the cards and can bully the Republicans. In his State of the Union speech in January, 1998, the president said that the first priority for the budget surplus must be to protect Social Security. "Save Social Security first," he said, over and over. But he still had not put out a detailed plan by the end of 1999.

Clinton's lack of specificity has created an opportunity for the Republicans, and there are two schools of thought on how to handle it.

One is to counter his move by saying, "We're going to protect Social Security, too," and not change anything. If he pledges to guarantee 60 percent of the budget surplus for Social Security, we're going to pledge 100 percent. That's exactly how the party's leaders reacted immediately to Clinton, and they haven't changed. Neither have they gotten much traction.

The other school of thought, percolating among some of the younger members of Congress, is to come up with the beginnings of reform—real reform.

The simple facts are these: Social Security will go into the red sometime in the not so distant future. (The date many experts cite is 2014.) That is, more money will be paid out than taken in. So there are three options for how to handle that. Option 1 is to decrease benefits. Option 2 is to increase taxes. Option 3 is to take the money out of the general fund (the revenue raised to run the government). Neither party has addressed this; professional politicians never address this sort of thing. They just talk about saving Social Security by not imposing a tax increase and not cutting benefits—in other words, not doing anything.

There is a lot of talk about a "surplus" in the "Social Security trust fund," but few people realize that in truth, there is no trust fund and that the surplus is an accounting illusion.

What has been happening is best explained by using a homely analogy. Say a guy gets a moonlighting job. The money from the moonlighting job is supposed to be saved so that he and his wife have a nest egg after they retire. So he comes home from his first week frying hamburgers at his moonlighting job. He's got the paycheck, and his wife says, "You know, we need shoes for the kids; we need a valve job on the car; we need a paint job on the house. I'm going to have to spend that money. I'm going to put an IOU in the desk drawer saying I took the money and spent it." That's what we've been doing with Social Security. The "trust fund" is a desk drawer full of nonnegotiable IOUs (called special issue bonds and bearing a very low interest rate), which are supposed to be exchanged for payroll tax receipts when the revenue is adequate.

President Clinton has a Rube Goldberg invention—very complex, very confusing (intentionally so)—on how to resuscitate the IOUs by turning them into ready cash. In brief, the special issue bonds (IOUs) would be turned in for regular Treasury notes. Thus, the trust fund would now contain

Treasuries, which would result in debt reduction as these securities are redeemed.

But wait. David Walker, the comptroller general of the United States, has testified that the Clinton plan actually spends more from the surplus and results in less debt reduction than if absolutely nothing were done. He also had this to say about the president's plan: "His approach . . . is extremely complex and confusing. This complexity and the confusion associated with it may serve to undercut the public's understanding of, and confidence in, the government's approach to budgeting and Social Security reform." Walker's words carry extra weight because even though he is a Republican, he is mandated by law to act in a nonpartisan manner.

It is truly hard to understand. I had breakfast in 1999 with a young Republican congressman, who told me that he was stunned to learn that most of his colleagues have no idea how Social Security works. The GOP has its work cut out for it in trying to explain to the people the true nature of the problem and of the solution regarding Social Security.

Hovering over the entire debate is the myth of Social Security as an insurance system. When Franklin Roosevelt set up the current system in the 1930s, he sold it to the American people as a collection of personal accounts: you paid in your "premiums" as you worked and drew down your "pension" after you retired. But when the system went into effect in 1938, it was financed as a pay-as-you-go system, with current workers paying for current retirees.

There are no personal accounts drawing interest. In 1999, I asked the Social Security people to send me a status of my "account." What I received was a list of my contributions dating back to 1946 when I was fifteen years old—except for the years I was in the army, when I made no contributions—and my contributions up to now. So, in this long life I had contributed $59,567. How much interest had it drawn? Nobody knows, because it isn't in any fund. It is $59,567—in 1946 dollars, in 1999 dollars, in in-between dollars. How much it really is, nobody has the faintest idea. It is the most God-awful accounting system possible. Of course, if I were to retire now (at age sixty-eight), the $59,567 in current dollars would be wiped out in about three years. But since it's a pay-as-you-go system, I'll receive full benefits even if I live to be one hundred. And if I died now, I would not receive one cent. It's not really my money!

The other uncomfortable reality of Social Security is the payroll tax that finances it. Every working person in America (with a few exceptions like active-duty military personnel and members of Congress) pays 15.3 percent of his or her earnings to Social Security and Medicare. This is on top of the income taxes that are levied by the federal and state governments. Moreover, the payroll tax is capped at $70,000, which means that the tax doesn't apply to income above that level, a restriction that benefits the rich more than the poor and the middle class. In fact, many working people pay more in payroll taxes than they pay in income taxes.

I would like to see the payroll tax eliminated and its revenue replaced by the national sales tax I discussed in the previous section. I recognize that this would mean discarding once and for all the myth of Social Security's being an insurance system, but it would be fairer in the long run than the system we've got right now. And it would be good politics for the Republican party. After all, how could the Republicans hope to abolish the income tax, which falls disproportionately on the rich, while not touching this oppressive and hated tax that falls most heavily on everybody else?

There is, however, a less radical approach that requires less political audacity.

• • •

The payroll tax and the insurance myth have served to block a lot of earlier attempts at reform, by Democrats and Republicans alike, especially because the elderly voters and the unions are so opposed to any changes in the existing system. It's not for nothing that Social Security is called "the third rail of American politics: touch it and you die."

But if a Republican leader is courageous enough to take the heat, there is a practical and potentially winning way to tackle the problem of Social Security's going broke in 2014. A few people have begun talking about this, but it needs a high-level endorsement to make it work. The idea is to take 2 percentage points off the 15.3 percent payroll tax, and instead of giving those 2 percentage points to the Treasury, give it to the taxpayer. He can't buy a Corvette with it (much as I'd like that); he has to put it in an equity fund of some kind, a retirement fund, that he can't touch until he's sixty-five years old. He can have an aggressive fund; he can have a passive fund; he can have a bond fund; he can pick from a limited menu of conservative investment options. He makes the choice. And every month, he gets a statement on how his fund is doing.

Democratic Senator Daniel Patrick Moynihan of New York has proposed a version of this, calling it a tax cut. It's not a tax cut. But there are people, including Republicans, who feel that if you give this to the taxpayer, he will think of the payroll tax as less than a tax. He will think of the payroll tax as less onerous than it was because he'll be seeing some of it, in an actual account that has his name on it, whereas before it went to the government and he didn't see that money at all. And, unlike Social Security, it actually would be his money.

This arrangement would have the effect of greatly reducing the bankruptcy problem for Social Security, because the funds would be producing so much more money that we would not have to reduce benefits in order for the system to be solvent after 2014. The better that these "2 percent funds" perform, the smaller the burden on the government will be. Think of how much money would be in my Social Security "account" if I could have invested a portion of my taxes in equities. I'll tell you this: the government would have a lot more than $59,567 to pay for my retirement benefits.

Of course, it would be better if all the funds from the payroll tax—the entire 15.3 percent—were invested at the discretion of the taxpayer, privatizing the entire system. But the 2 percent plan is a start.

Do the Republicans have the guts to take this approach? I don't have much faith in the Republican Congress, which has backed away from giving the budget surplus back in tax cuts and can't be expected to take a courageous position. Nothing happened in 1999, and that meant nothing in the election year of 2000.

It's going to have to be left for a Republican president to do the heavy lifting. Senate Majority Leader Trent Lott's long-standing position is, in effect, "I will not jump off the Social Security bridge unless I am hand in hand with Bill Clinton and we jump off together"—which means he will not change the system unless Clinton goes along. And Clinton, with all of his meandering rhetoric, will not privatize Social Security, even by this very modest 2 percent program.

On this issue, the Democrats have been completely inflexible. Some of the moderate Democratic congressmen have told me that, yes, we can have a little bit of private investment—not from the payroll tax but from the budget surplus. Their condition is that the investment decisions have to be made by the government, just as President Clinton proposed. In other words, you cannot direct how this money will be invested; the government will decide.

I asked John Zogby to conduct a poll on that issue, which showed substantial opposition to the government's making such decisions—58.1 percent to 28.9 percent—saying that the decision for investment should be made by the individual citizens. That included even higher support from African Americans (59.9 percent), Hispanics (69.4 percent), women working outside the home (66.5 percent), union members (64.3 percent), and those under age thirty (74.8 percent).

There's a lot of potential public support, but no courage within the GOP—no courage to touch the third rail and live. The Republicans remember past campaigns. They remember how Clinton terrified elderly voters on the Medicare issue in 1995 and 1996 and how the Democrats more ferociously attacked Ronald Reagan on Social Security in the 1982 midterm elections. They're terribly frightened by this. They have even barred the use of the word *privatize*.

In the spring of 1999, the Republican plan put forth by the two senior members of the House Ways and Means Committee, Chairman Bill Archer of Texas and Clay Shaw of Florida, had business-as-usual stamped over it. Two percentage points of payroll would be given to the individual to invest in a list of options, but the money would come not from the payroll tax but from the general fund! What's more, when a person retired, all the money accumulated under this investment would go back into the Social Security pot. Admittedly, this is a plan to save Social Security, not to reform it. More specifically, it is a self-serving plan to get a piece of paper from the program's financing administration saying that the Republicans have a plan to guarantee continuation of the pension payments.

What the Republicans need is a presidential candidate from outside Washington who is not afraid of reform and is willing to explain it to the public. Most of all, it has to be explained to voters over age sixty-five that this reform has absolutely no impact on them. It's for people who will retire after 2014—those now in their twenties, thirties, and forties. Most of the Republican candidates are age fifty-five or younger, and I firmly believe that they can appeal to younger voters on this issue without alienating their parents' generation.

The beauty—and poetic justice—of the 2 percent plan is that just as Social Security established a base of support for the New Deal coalition that lasted long after the 1930s, this plan can similarly propel Republican support into the future. Consider the political impact if there is a sheet of paper in the mail that comes once a month showing how much money is in your account. What this would do, in effect, would be to steal Franklin Roosevelt's playbook from the Democrats by giving individuals a personal stake in the new system.

The beginning of any meaningful reform is some kind of plan converting part of the payroll tax into personal accounts. It is not an option for Republicans to play it safe (as is their inclination) by saying, "We're going to take this off the board for the 2000 campaign." If a GOP presidential candidate is willing to take the heat from the left, he can do what FDR did for the Democrats sixty years ago and capture working people for the Republican party of the future.

More than mere tactics is at stake here. Whether the Republicans have the courage to go down this road may determine the course of politics in America.

Stop Reflexively Opposing Campaign Finance Reform

Campaign finance reform is one of those issues that the Democrats will seek to capitalize on in 2000, targeting Republicans for resisting any change at all to the current system. It's very much like the tax issue. If the Republicans don't have an alternative to present, they play into the Democrats' hands.

Making the Republican timidity on this issue worse, the Democrats are drenched in hypocrisy. Early in 1999, Ceci Connolly of *The Washington Post* reported that Vice President Al Gore, in getting ready for his 2000 presidential campaign, "plans to exploit every available legal loophole to collect far more money than the basic spending limits allow." Yet it's hard for Republicans to condemn this hypocrisy when they are immobilized on campaign finance reform—saying nothing, doing nothing, trying their best to block everything.

The Republicans need to emerge from their total opposition to any serious reform because signs are that they will suffer for it. They fought a losing battle in the House in 1998 while managing to stop action in the Senate, but they entered the current Congress with less confidence that they could continue to prevail. So instead of being back on their heels fighting, they would have been much better off to try and devise a workable plan of their own. Being anti-everything cannot help the Republican cause.

• • •

In the campaign finance fights after the Republicans took control of Congress in 1994, the Democrats vigorously pressed for the limitation of all kinds of campaign contributions—except those from organized labor, which, of course, is very good for them. (This followed little or no interest by Democratic leaders in the 1970s and 1980s, when they controlled Congress.) The Republicans, after some tossing and turning to find a rationale for the existing system, which they saw as giving them an advantage, seized on the First Amendment with this argument: Contributing money to a political campaign is a form of speech, and it is unconstitutional to limit free speech. The Supreme Court basically endorsed this view in *Buckley* v. *Valeo* (1976), and it remains the law of the land.

Court rulings and constitutional arguments notwithstanding, my sense is that people are appalled by the state of campaign finance in America today. Is this an issue that disturbs them night after night, day after day? Certainly not. But you have a situation where the Republicans, who put themselves forward as a reform party in 1994, look less and less like a reform party by stonewalling on this issue. (Their backsliding on term limits hasn't helped either, as I will discuss later.)

If the Republicans are truly going to change the system of government—less government, less spending, less regulation—they had better have clean hands. That means they cannot be seen as the lackeys of special interests that will benefit from these changes. And to have clean hands, they have to propose a meaningful change in the way we finance campaigns.

The system now in place, which was created by the 1974 campaign reforms in reaction to Watergate, is a classic case of unintended consequences. That law's rigid, nonindexed $1,000 limit on contributions has made it difficult to finance a campaign, because $1,000 today is obviously quite different from what $1,000 was twenty-five years ago (amounting to $3,300 in 1999 money)—not only because of inflation, but because television is a much more important part of the equation than it was back then.

If it were up to me, I'd remove the limits altogether. But that won't happen. On the other hand, the loopholes in the current system, permitting so-called soft money, (unlimited contributions can come in so long as the money isn't spent on a particular candidate's campaign), has created a tremendous slush fund of special-interest cash. The 1974 law also spawned political action committees (PACs), which became another means to increase the influence of special interests in federal elections.

One Republican who has tried to stake out a reformist position is Senator John McCain of Arizona, who joined forces with Democratic Senator Russell Feingold of Wisconsin to sponsor a comprehensive campaign finance bill in 1998. A big problem with the McCain-Feingold bill is that McCain, in his eagerness to get campaign reform passed, bought into what could be called the union waiver: Labor PACs are effectively exempted from the limits imposed on business and industry PACs, which tilts the playing field unfairly to the Democrats' advantage. If the unions don't get hurt very much, then it's not really reform. In 1999, McCain said he would insist on new labor union restrictions, specifically a variant of "paycheck protection" to bar involuntary checkoffs for labor's political contributions (while adding that the same protection should apply to corporate shareholders). But McCain should have reached this point much earlier.

The question is, can the two parties put together something that really hits on labor?

Representative Linda Smith of Washington State was a conservative Republican who favored campaign finance reform, and as such, she was "adopted" by a left-leaning coalition put together by Common Cause. When she advocated paycheck protection, Republicans immediately endorsed the idea. Her new Democratic and liberal friends dropped her flat.

Nor did the Republican endorsement of paycheck protection manifest a serious endorsement of reform. Senate Majority Leader Trent Lott and his close ally, Senator Mitch McConnell of Kentucky, made clear that their amendments to McCain-Feingold limiting labor PACs were meant to be "poison pills." They were not intended to improve the bill, but to kill it by forcing the Democrats to vote against the entire reform. They said this openly, thereby conceding that they're not very serious about finding a way to real reform.

McConnell, the chairman of the Republican Senatorial Campaign Committee, has taken a maximalist position in refusing to countenance any change in the current system. Even his rhetoric is apocalyptic: "Take away 'soft money' and we wouldn't be in the majority in the House and the majority in the Senate and couldn't win back the White House," he said in April 1999. "Hell's going to freeze over before we get rid of soft money."

I just can't agree with him. Are Republican ideas so unpopular that the party must rely on an increasingly suspect system of raising money to keep itself in power? I'm not prepared to cede the high ground to the Democrats, and neither should any conservative. Granted, provisions of the original McCain-Feingold (before it was watered down in October 1999)—restricting voting guides rating members of Congress and limiting public utterances by private groups in the closing weeks of a campaign—went much too far and were skewed against conservatives. But by taking an intransigent position, Republicans take themselves out of the game.

There is a small but growing number of Republicans who say that although the system we have of financing may produce a lot of Republican money, it is not helping the Republican party as much as people like Lott and McConnell think.

Linda Smith was a lonely conservative Republican reformer during her four years in Congress (1995–1998). She proposed to limit campaign contributions to come solely from the state or district of the contested election, so that candidates no longer would be able to run to New York and California for the big money. That idea previously was suggested by the influential Vin Weber, a congressman-turned-lobbyist serving on a Republican campaign finance advisory board, but it generated no interest from either party.

This would be a valuable reform in cleaning up politics. The purists say that it hurts the First Amendment, but I don't know how pure they really are. From what I can see, they are the ones benefiting from the current system, and they can't see the bigger picture of how it is hurting the Republican party and its cause.

Chuck Hagel, an interesting young first-term senator from

Nebraska, has said that the system has to change. It didn't help the Republican party all that much in 1992 or 1996, he says, and the party will have to clean up this system if it is going to regain the high ground.

Hagel was encouraged by a lot of people in the Senate Republican caucus, including some very senior committee chairmen, to run against McConnell's reelection as chairman of the campaign committee. They argued that somebody had to take the blame for failing to win Senate seats in 1998. Since they did not feel comfortable trying to punish Lott for failing to establish a Republican agenda in his leadership of the Senate, it had to be McConnell. He had raised piles of money to no other purpose than burnishing the GOP's money-grubbing reputation.

But when Hagel ran, he got only nineteen out of fifty-five votes. Welcome to Washington! This proved yet again how hard it is to accomplish reform within the culture of the congressional parties.

•   •   •

Campaign finance reform represents an important opportunity for the Republicans, but it would have to be done by somebody outside Washington who could stand behind a plan that really did reform the system and without a clear benefit for either side. It would have to restrict labor, but it would also have to restrict soft money from corporations.

Let me be clear: It's not going to be easy to bring around the party leadership to this point of view after all these years. It's all a matter of how much the Republicans want to be a real radical reform party. The voters are looking more and more for candidates with clean hands, and to have clean hands, the Republicans have to get rid of this PAC/soft-money system.

I think there's a lot of merit to that position. It would make for a better system, and it would help the Republicans in the presidential campaign if they could say that they had taken anti-regulatory, low-tax positions not because they are getting big PAC checks, but because they believe in the merits of their case.

I also think the Republicans would be well advised to come out against all the subsidies that parties and candidates receive from the government. Consider the $3 checkoff for financing the presidential campaign that's on everyone's federal income tax form. Every year, the number of people who say that they want their money to go to financing elections keeps declining: from 27.5 percent in 1976, when the checkoff began, to 12.5 percent in 1997, the last available year of IRS statistics. The percentage drops a little every year.

But Congress keeps appropriating the money, and a lot of people don't know that there is a very heavy subsidy through this $3 checkoff for the conventions of both parties: $12 million for each national convention. The Republicans obviously don't want to give up that money, but I think it would be a good political move—even daring—for them to do so. They might have to hold a slightly less glitzy convention, but they would come across as a reform-type party. There were hints that they might take that step in 1996, but they never reached fruition.

I know that historically it is uncharacteristic for the Republicans to be a reform party, but they are confronted with a great opportunity if they choose to seize it. A reform party appeals to swing voters, who respect politicians who put their money where their mouth is. And the GOP should not ignore the Reform party constituency—voters attracted to candidates as dissimilar as Ross Perot, Jesse Ventura, and Pat Buchanan who call for the existing system to be demolished.

The reason that campaign finance reform is good for the Republicans in 2000 is not so much that there is an army of voters who are waiting to be energized by campaign finance reform itself, but because the lack of reform limits the Republicans' ability to engage the red-meat issues that will get their voters to the polls. Senators Lott and McConnell may pride themselves on stopping, at least temporarily, the flawed McCain-Feingold bill, but the party may not be able to survive more victories of this sort.

Once again, it comes down to a courageous stand by the presidential candidate. There is a glimmer of hope in 2000 because two of the candidates (George W. Bush and Steve Forbes) will refuse to accept federal matching funds, which means that they will not be bound by federal spending limits. Bush and Forbes have so much money on hand that they can afford to opt out personally from the matching funds, meaning that they have literal capital as well as political capital to spend on taking a courageous stand in favor of true and equitable campaign finance reform. And probably only the party's presidential nominee can do it.

•   •   •

Congress is compromised by the pervasive role and influence of lobbyists in Washington. Ordinary people probably don't understand how the system really works. They might think the lobbyist for the Screw Manufacturers of America has an agenda, he peddles the agenda, and he gives a congressman a $1,000 check occasionally to help lubricate it.

The reality is quite different. Lobbyists are an integral part of the inner workings of politics. They sit in on strategy sessions; they are particularly involved in campaign finance. Every major presidential candidate of either party has people in the lobbyist community attending his planning sessions. A high-powered lobbyist firm, if it's a Republican firm, will have a person involved in each prospective nominee's campaign and raising money for those campaigns. If it's a bipartisan firm, it's going to have representatives in both parties.

George W. Bush, for example, early in 1999 called for "Pioneers"—people who would promise to raise $100,000 each for the campaign. Only a lobbyist is likely to know enough potential contributors to raise $100,000 in contributions no larger than $1,000 per person. The lobbyist-Pioneer, pledging $100,000, goes down to Austin, and even though he may not meet Bush, he certainly gets to meet the people around him and makes invaluable contacts. The lobbyists are intimately and inextricably involved in this whole campaign finance issue. Within a few weeks, there were 260 Pioneers—and more on the way. If they all come through on their promises, that amounts to a cool $26 million.

This process is not a good thing—not for the country or for the party. As I mentioned before, the economist Milton Friedman often has said that we will never be able to reform the tax code because the lobbyist industry has a symbiotic relationship with the politicians: the lobbyists give the contributions to the congressmen, and the congressmen do the bidding of the lobbyists. Just as there is a built-in constituency on the Hill against tax reform, the same is true regarding campaign finance reform.

To break their hold on Congress, we have to get limitations on PACs in congressional and presidential campaigns. And if we can have some kind of restriction that 70 or 80 percent of the money must be raised within the state or district of the public official, this would greatly reduce the impact of the lobbyists on legislation and on the priorities of the Republican party.

Because of the influence of lobbyists, Republicans wind up having problems enacting meaningful tax reform, which is probably the best issue for them. And the lobbyists also stand in the way of term limits, another good issue for the GOP that I'll discuss later.

These are very resonant issues with the public that never get exploited. Conversely, Republicans demur from the necessary reforms that are desired by business, such as tort reform and environmental deregulation, because of the mere appearance that they are on the take. That was the main reason that Linda Smith (who was nominated for Congress in 1994 on a write-in) pledged to cheering delegates at the Ross Perot convention in Dallas in the summer of 1995 that she would clean up the campaign finance mess. A few months later, she was deeply depressed.

"If you don't stop the flow of money to Congress," Smith told me that autumn, "people will think that everything we do is attached back to the money of the special interests. I've been here ten months, and I'm fed up. I see many of my freshman friends getting used to the stink—forgetting what they came here for." She told me that Newt Gingrich and the other Republican leaders had lied to her when they promised campaign reform. Gingrich was furious when her quotes appeared in my newspaper column.

By 1997, the Republicans had solidly turned against campaign reform, accepting Mitch McConnell's argument that losing the millions of dollars would mean electoral disaster for the GOP, and Linda Smith was a pariah. In 1998, in the midst of a losing campaign for the Senate where the support given her by campaign chairman McConnell was lukewarm at best, she accused Republican leaders of holding up action on a bill in order to milk more campaign contributions. "Isn't that extortion?" she asked.

Corporate lobbyists wanted nothing to do with Smith, or with her unsuccessful 1998 Senate campaign against liberal Democratic Senator Patty Murray. Neither did conservative voting groups, despite her flawless voting record for their positions. She had a perfect score in opposing abortion, but the National Right to Life Committee did not endorse her because she supported campaign reform (although the organization's state committee in Washington did back her). Conversely, the national committee supported members of Congress with flawed abortion records because they opposed campaign reform. It was a classic case of Republicans and their supporters confusing what they had come to Washington to achieve.

Embrace Global Free Markets

The issue of foreign trade has split both parties, but the Republicans have the chance to come out better positioned than the Democrats if they keep their focus where it belongs.

What is most striking about this issue is the massive, dramatic change in sides that has taken place in the twentieth century. Traditionally the Democrats were the free-trade party, and the Republicans were the party of protection. When William McKinley was chairman of the House Ways and Means Committee, he was the author of the landmark McKinley Tariff Act, and the slogan of his 1896 presidential campaign was "Patriotism, Prosperity, and Protection." And it worked very well as he won two terms as president. It was not until Dwight D. Eisenhower that the Republicans made the switch on trade. For a brief spell, both parties were for free trade, and then the Democrats increasingly veered toward becoming the party of protection going into the 1970s and 1980s, thanks to organized labor, as their answer to globalization and competition abroad.

In modern times, however, protectionism has been a losing issue. Candidates who have tried to build their campaigns around it have gotten great applause lines—and very few votes.

John B. Connally is a classic example. He was a former governor of Texas, a former secretary of the treasury, an intimate adviser of both Lyndon B. Johnson and Richard M. Nixon who switched parties from Democrat to Republican in the early 1970s. Connally was a truly commanding figure on the national scene who ran for the Republican presidential nomination in 1980 against George Bush and Ronald Reagan, and he got enthusiastic crowd response when he talked about the last worker in America sweeping out a McDonald's hamburger joint. In the end, though, he won only one delegate, despite spending $13.7 million (a huge figure for 1980) on his campaign.

Four years later, in 1984, former Vice President Walter Mondale started off his run for the Democratic nomination with a strong protectionist line. But after reading a few polls on the subject, he pulled back sharply from that strong position in no time. Protectionism just doesn't work.

Before Pat Buchanan reinvented himself as the champion of protectionism during his first campaign for president in 1992—after avowing free-trade orthodoxy as an aide to Presidents Nixon and Reagan—the most successful candidate to advocate trade restrictions (if you could call him truly successful) was Representative Richard Gephardt, who competed against Michael Dukakis, Al Gore, Jesse Jackson, and others for the Democratic nomination in 1988.

I remember having dinner with Gephardt's campaign manager in Des Moines that year. He laid out for me the appeal that Gephardt was making—that basically the people were being wiped out by globalization. I said that he was appealing to the losers in the economy, and, I added, there just aren't that many losers today. Remember, this was 1988 and times were pretty good, before the so-called Bush recession of the early 1990s. And he replied, "We will make them *feel* like they're losers" (which I thought was a great line and more revealing about the Democratic party's philosophy than he may have realized).

Four years later, Pat Buchanan started off preaching the pure Republican religion against the Bush apostasy, but he also ended up appealing to the losers in society. Not many losers are Republicans proportionally, which is why Buchanan ran into problems down the road. There were enough people hurting in states that were going through hard times, specifically New Hampshire, where he ran surprisingly well against President Bush in 1992 and then won the 1996 primary. Beginning the 2000 election cycle, he campaigned as the only Republican candidate stressing the trade issue, which still served him well in Weirton, West Virginia, where the old steel mill is endangered by foreign competition (and where Buchanan began his third presidential campaign in 1999), but not in most of the country.

At the time of the Weirton announcement, strategists of the Republican party and the Bush campaign thought that Buchanan's time had come and gone—a victim of the nation's general prosperity. Much of his 1996 staff had been hired by Steve Forbes. The anti-abortion movement's support was spread among several candidates. But in the late summer of 1999, Buchanan became a menace to Republican hopes for 2000 as he moved to bolt the GOP and become the presidential nominee of Ross Perot's Reform party. He argued that his beloved Republican party had become a "Xerox copy" of the Democrats on questions of world economics that now preoccupied him. The justification was that the party establishment supporting a "new world order" had rigged the nomination in favor of George W. Bush.

Born and bred a Republican whose total career of public service had been as an aide to Richard Nixon and later Ronald Reagan, Buchanan was moving into strange company in the Reform ranks. Perot's hostility to Republicans and especially to the Bushes was palpable. Washington consultant Pat Choate, Perot's 1996 running mate, was closely tied to Minority Leader Richard Gephardt and other House Democrats. Lenora Fulani ran for president in 1988 as an independent, advocating a radical left-wing agenda. Buchanan had collaborated with them all in 1993–1994 to oppose the NAFTA agreement, and all they had in common now was opposition to globalism and its free trade precepts embodied in NAFTA, GATT, and the World Trade Organization.

As he was considering the possibility of abandoning the GOP, Buchanan described to me the American economy as "the marvel of the world" but warned that the burgeoning trade deficit "is not sustainable. For a mature nation, it means that the nation is in a state of decline." Such Cassandra-like warnings of impending doom were not likely to generate strong electoral support in 2000 and, in any event, might well attract as many Democratic voters as Republicans. What worried Republicans for the short-term was the possibility that hard-core Republican voters, unhappy with the collapse of the Gingrich revolution for reasons unrelated to global economics, would turn to Buchanan in sufficient numbers in November to elect a Democrat.

• • •

I can't imagine that any politician really believes that protectionism by itself is a winning issue right now. As long as the economy is relatively stable and more people are winners than losers, free trade is an issue that the Republicans don't have to be ashamed of and don't have to back away from.

Unfortunately, the party is badly divided on trade (as on much else). The Republicans in Congress after the 1998 election said with some pride they would no longer supply Clinton the votes today for NAFTA, even though that's what they did when it passed in 1993. In fact, a vastly higher percentage of Republicans than Democrats voted in favor of the free-trade agreement with Mexico and Canada. In 1998, they refused to supply Clinton the votes on "fast-track" authority, which would restore to the president the power to submit trade treaties to the Senate for a straight up-or-down vote—a power that all presidents since Gerald Ford had enjoyed, until the law lapsed in 1998, and is essential if the United States is to negotiate international trade agreements. If the Democrats would not supply the votes for their own president, asked the Republicans, why should they?

But their opposition to Bill Clinton should not blind them to the fact that free trade is a great opportunity for the Republicans, particularly since the labor union domination of the Democratic party is such that they cannot think clearly on this issue. The protectionist dogma is pervasive in the Democratic party, and it will hurt Democrats at the polls, well into the future.

●   ●   ●

The Clinton administration has tried to present itself as zealous in its promotion of free-trade agreements that open new markets, but the reality is much more ambiguous. President Clinton is very political, and at the same time that he practiced free trade, he was trying to protect his labor flank.

That's why he didn't push very hard on "fast track" starting in 1997.

He can say he's for "fast track," but he has not put on the campaign he put on for NAFTA in 1993, because he doesn't want to push labor too far—and neither does Vice President Gore. They want to be very careful here and not antagonize their strongest ally. The Democratic party cannot do without the ground troops of organized labor.

Sure, the president appeared to come out for "fast track" in his 1999 State of the Union, but he did it sotto voce— never even saying those two little words. It was Clinton at his super-slick trickiest. Raising his voice, the president declared: "We must enforce our trade laws when imports unlawfully flood our nation. [Applause.] I have already informed the government of Japan that if that nation's sudden surge of steel imports into our country is not reversed, American will respond. [Standing ovation.]" With that macho protectionist display out of the way, the president quietly called for a "a new round of global trade negotiations to expand exports of services, manufacturers and farm products"—something that needs "fast-track" legislation.

In fact, he didn't do anything on either front: nothing on "fast track," nothing to stop dumping steel either. So it's a finesse operation.

Al Gore is going to have to be very careful on all these issues. I don't think we're going to see him press very hard for more free-trade agreements before the 2000 election. And if he's elected president, who knows what he'll be doing? I firmly believe that this is a blow-out deal for Republicans if they want to take a strong free-trade position. They have little to lose and a lot to gain, because free trade appeals to the winners in society—in other words, their core constituency.

•   •   •

Another trade issue that could play a role in a Republican campaign in 2000 grows out of the Asian financial crisis that began in 1997 and the Mexican bailout a few years before that. The Clinton administration took the position that in times of trouble, the United States must prop up our trading partners with loan guarantees and other help.

This is a "moral hazard" question, meaning that by trying to help someone, you may inadvertently encourage more of the bad behavior that caused the problem in the first place. A country or bank that makes a risky investment and then gets bailed out may continue to make bad investments in the future on the assumption that it will get bailed out again if things go wrong. I think that situations like these present another opportunity for the Republicans to show what might be called a semipopulist position by saying, "Look, part of investing is risk, and sometimes people lose money."

In all fairness, presidents of both parties have been locked into the global financial establishment, including the International Monetary Fund and the World Bank. That means they end up being in favor of bailouts in all cases. For the twelve years of the Reagan and Bush administrations, Republicans were strongly in favor of the IMF against the screams of protests of people like Pat Buchanan (including during his period as an aide in Ronald Reagan's White House). In 1990, after a visit to Latin America, Vice President Dan Quayle told President Bush and key cabinet members over lunch that the IMF was supplying a "suicide pill" for the region's fledgling democracies. When I reported Quayle's remarks in the Evans-Novak column, the vice president was informed by the White House to say no more about the IMF, and he complied.

Indeed, all incumbent presidents tend to support the IMF. Former Federal Reserve Governor Lawrence Lindsey, a strong critic of the IMF, went down to Texas late in 1998 for his first visit with George W. Bush prior to putting together an economic advisory team for Governor Bush's presidential candidacy. When Lindsey advised the governor to take a strong, critical position against what the IMF does, Bush was taken aback and said, "Aren't these just the nuts who are opposed to this?" The education of George W. Bush began apace, and it promises to be very interesting.

But the more important point is this: On this particular element of globalization, the Republican party should take a position that is more in line with Pat Buchanan—that bailouts are counterproductive and that the IMF does more harm than good. The Mexican bailout of 1994–1995 was a mistake, and the idea of providing more U.S. taxpayer funds to the IMF is wrong.

I think that this issue has strong populist appeal, and it's extremely difficult for the Clinton administration to defend itself here. Robert Rubin, the much-celebrated former secretary of the treasury, was an uncompromising supporter of the IMF. This represents an opportunity for the Republicans, especially if Al Gore is the Democratic nominee. And it's not only just straight politics; the IMF has made matters worse by prescribing austerity policies as the condition for aid to these countries, which in fact inhibits rather than encourages economic growth.

It's not easy, considering the symbiotic relationship of congressmen and lobbyists. When the Republican Congress in 1998 delayed authorization of additional IMF spending, big business and its agents in Washington put on the pressure, and the GOP leadership finally capitulated and passed the bill.

A Republican candidate will have to be willing to take the heat from global corporations and banks and from the Washington lobbyists who are representing these businesses. But then the party could make real headway on this populist issue—so long as it doesn't jump headlong into full-blown protectionism.

•   •   •

The kind of voters who don't need any prompting to be outraged by the IMF—and who would not have been surprised by the revelation in the late summer of 1999 that billions of dollars in American taxpayer's money had been funneled through that agency to finance corruption in Russia—will also be responsive to attacks on the Federal Reserve. But there are probably not enough of them to make such attacks pay politically as a campaign issue in 2000.

The nation's central bank has a peculiar political history. Created in 1913 as part of President Woodrow Wilson's progressive agenda, it became the citadel of Wall Street conservatism—attacked by the left and defended by the right. But beginning in the late 1970s, the supply-side movement, as defined by Arthur Laffer and Jude Wanniski and orchestrated by Jack Kemp, tried to introduce monetary policy as a political issue by calling on the Fed to target the price of gold.

It proved a flop politically when Kemp advocated the gold standard as the bulwark of a stable economy to baffled Iowa farmers in his ill-fated 1988 campaign for president. But as Republican hopefuls campaigned in Iowa in 1999, the Fed and monetary policy again emerged as an issue. In response to the recent Asian financial crisis, the central bank had lowered interest rates in 1998. That same year it bailed out Long-Term Capital Management, a financial house (whose partners included former Federal Reserve vice chairman David Mullins) that had overextended itself with risky overseas investments.

Yet, in 1999, despite ruinously low farm prices (and a low price of gold), the Fed under Chairman Alan Greenspan was raising interest rates to keep leashed the inflationary dogs. Actually, there was no sign of inflation, but the Fed wanted to cool what Greenspan called "irrational exuberance," reflected by a stock market reaching record highs.

Greenspan, who had been named to the Fed by President Reagan in 1987 and reappointed by Presidents Bush and Clinton, was an icon on Wall Street—particularly for bond traders. But in Iowa, GOP candidates Steve Forbes, Dan Quayle, Gary Bauer, and Pat Buchanan assailed Greenspan for protecting the interests of Wall Street, not Main Street. The prospective nominee—George W. Bush—staunchly defended him.

Can Fed-bashing be a winning issue for Republicans? Probably not. It is too arcane to enunciate on the political stump for a mass audience even if what is done behind closed doors at the Federal Reserve's marble palace on Constitution Avenue is of vital importance to the American economy.

• • •

In the final analysis, it's important to remember that there is a very small constituency against globalization, even though it is very vocal, especially on the radio call-in programs. There has to be a Republican will to appeal to a broader national sentiment on trade. They don't have the problem that the Democrats have. The Democrats' most important foot soldiers are in organized labor, and organized labor is adamant on this issue. That's why organized labor delayed until October 1999 its endorsement of Gore's candidacy—to make sure he would be with them on the issue. They did not want him going off the reservation.

Even though this is probably not an issue that by itself wins the election, I still think this is an opportunity. It is a plus issue for the Republicans, and as the nonincumbent party in a presidential contest, the Republicans need to avail themselves of all the plus issues at their disposal.

Welcome the Religious Conservatives as a Force for Good

One of the most striking things I have noticed over the past several years is that when I speak to establishment Republicans, the first thing they say to me is not, "What are we going to do about Bill Clinton?" but, "What are we going to do about these right wingers?" as they call the religious conservatives. In a nastier tone, they also often refer to them as "wackos" and "full-mooners." There is an enormous hostility toward them within the Republican party itself, which I think is very damaging. The message has been put out by a lot of the establishment people that the religious conservatives are not wanted.

When the Republican National Committee met in Palm Springs, California, in 1998, "Team 100"—the people who give $100,000 a year to the party—was meeting in the same place at the same time. These big contributors are among the most unforgiving opponents of the Christian conservatives. Just watching them getting on their bus and getting off, and watching the Christian conservative members of the RNC eye them with a malevolent gaze, I could tell from their dress alone that these are two different worlds. They are culturally quite different. I think that helps explain the intensity of the opposition. The country club Republicans also have bought into the news media's depiction of religious conservatives as a dangerous force, leading the Republican party down a path it should not take.

The problem for the Republicans is a matter of rudimentary politics. They cannot be a majority party without the support of the Christian conservatives, and so they had better learn to live with them. And if they welcome the Christians instead of spurning them, they will find them to be a force for good, not evil.

•   •   •

Before 1980, religious conservatives tended to have a poorer voting record than most other groups in the country. In 1976 they had been lured into voting for Jimmy Carter, the first avowed born-again Christian to run for president, and they contributed to Carter's victory over Gerald Ford that year. But once in office, Carter showed himself to be, in political terms, less a born-again Christian than a typical liberal Democrat. The religious conservatives felt that he did not do any of the things they had thought he was going to do on abortion, the Equal Rights Amendment, homosexuals, or school prayer.

"I was thrilled at the thought of a born-again in the White House," said Dr. William W. Pennell, the pastor of the huge Forrest Hills Baptist Church in Decatur, Georgia, in 1980. He quickly added that the thrill was starting to fade by Inauguration Day, 1977, when Carter "mentioned the Lord's name less often than any other president." He also thought that Carter was very weak on foreign policy, saying, "I've had about all the born-again diplomacy I can stand."

What made Pennell's comments so noteworthy was that

he made them at an extraordinary meeting of some two hundred evangelical ministers in July 1980 that he hosted at his
church to consider Ronald Reagan's challenge to Carter in
that year's presidential election. He and the other assembled
divines were breaking new ground. Not only was such overt
participation in a political event unusual for white southern
preachers, but the presence of Paul Weyrich, a Washington-
based political activist who was a leader of what was called
the New Right, was a tip-off that the Decatur meeting had
national implications.

A former radio newsman from Wisconsin who had
switched from the Roman Catholic church to the Eastern
Rite Melkite church in protest against the English-language
liturgy authorized by Vatican II, Weyrich was a superb political organizer. The day-long Decatur meeting concluded with
nuts-and-bolts advice on how the pastors could urge their
flocks to vote Republican without losing tax exemptions for
their churches. Two more such sessions were held in Georgia, and then dozens more throughout the South. Simultaneously, the Moral Majority (the name was coined by Weyrich)
had been formed in Lynchburg, Virginia, by the Rev. Jerry
Falwell.

This unprecedented assistance from the pulpits of the
Bible Belt contributed to Reagan's onslaught on Carter's home
base and brought the religious conservatives firmly into the
Republican party, for whom they helped elect presidents in
1980, 1984, and 1988 and Congresses in 1994, 1996, and
1998.

So why was there so much hostility toward them within
the ranks of the GOP? Part of it was instilled by the forces
of the left in the culture war. The left controls the news
media, the entertainment industry, and the college campuses.

All of these people are highly secular, highly antagonistic toward religious feeling. Surveys have shown that Washington-based journalists register at the bottom of the scale among all occupation groups for religious devotion. They are not only hostile, but frightened by people of faith.

Moreover, the Democrats have absolutely blistered the Christian conservatives—and indeed, almost all conservatives—as the "far right," an epithet gleefully parroted by the mainstream news media and repeated by all too many Republicans, including conservatives. This is truly an outrage. I think of the far right as Adolf Hitler and his supporters: people who really hate democracy, despise freedom of religion and freedom of the press, oppose political opposition and open elections, and, of course, kill people they don't like. Ralph Reed, Pat Robertson, James Dobson, and Jerry Falwell, like them or not, surely are not part of the far right.

Nevertheless, the identification of these Christian conservatives as far-right extremists has become ingrained. It also has become holy writ for country club Republicans who would rather lose and keep control of the franchise than win and be on the outside. They just don't like these newcomers. (They are joined in their hostility by a lot of pro-choice Republican women who are single-minded about the abortion issue, which I will discuss later.)

The fact remains that since 1980, the Christian Coalition and the religious conservatives have become to the Republican party what organized labor is to the Democratic party. They are the foot soldiers, the heart of the party, the most dependable activists. The Republicans cannot win elections without them. They also bring the potential of a new force of voters coming in who were not previously Republicans, as they proved in 1980 and 1994. Social conservative leader Gary Bauer (and a 2000 presidential hopeful) is a great example of a religious conservative from a culturally Democratic family; his father, a janitor, was a lifelong, blue-collar Democrat. And there are many others like him.

The religious conservatives have proved themselves to be an absolutely devastating force in local elections. The country club Republicans complain, however, that while the Christians have proved that they can win primaries, they don't have the follow-through in general elections. For example, in a 1998 congressional primary in southern California, Brooks Firestone, a moderate, upper-class Republican hand-picked by Speaker Newt Gingrich, was defeated in the primary by Tom Bordonaro, a Christian conservative, who was in turn defeated by the Democrat in the general election.

What the moderates prefer not to see is that religious conservatives do win general elections. In 1994, a political outsider named Ron Lewis—a former steelworker and Baptist minister who ran a Christian bookstore in Elizabethtown, Kentucky—won a hotly contested race to represent Kentucky's 2nd District in Congress. He was the first Republican in 129 years to win that House seat, which had been held for the preceding forty-one years by Democrat William Natcher, chairman of the House Appropriations Committee.

The religious right is also very influential in deciding statewide elections. I really cannot imagine the Republicans carrying Congress again, or winning the presidential election, without active participation by the Christian conservatives. The apparent decline of the Christian Coalition after Ralph Reed departed as executive director following the 1996 election is no more important than the disappearance of the Moral Majority in 1997. Whatever the name of the umbrella organization, the religious conservatives are crucial to the GOP.

A lot of moderate Republicans—the ones who keep wishing the religious conservatives would just go away (though they don't explain who's going to do all the legwork in their place)—argue that the Republicans can't have a majority with the religious conservatives because voters in the middle will be scared off by them.

But from what I've seen around the country, the number of people who are really alienated by the evangelicals, and will vote for the Democrats instead, is relatively small. The Republican coalition does not include a lot of people who are left of center on the issues, and so there is nothing terrible to worry about here. The game plan for a Republican victory in 2000 has to include religious conservatives in full force, as they were in 1980 and 1994.

The bottom line is this: If the Republicans have an appealing message, then the different groups within the party—the country clubbers, the businesspeople, the religious conservatives—will all be able to coexist so long as they focus on something bigger. When there isn't something bigger, they tend to focus on each other. And the deeper strains in the party stem from the lack of an agenda in the 1998 election and the fuzzy agenda going into 2000. If the Republicans fix that problem, this nonproblem of the religious conservatives will fall into place.

•   •   •

That's not to say that the party can be complacent about the Christian conservatives. The Republicans have to do more than tolerate them; they have to welcome them into the fold.

Many religious conservatives do not have historic loyalties to the Republican party, so they can very easily walk away. It is therefore critical to remember not simply how valuable they are, but also how tenuous is their connection to the Republican party.

Republican rejection of the Christian activists is dangerous and shortsighted and plays into the hands of the Democrats down the road. They don't realize that in 1998, the vote by the Christian conservatives fell off, and partly as a result of that, the Republicans unexpectedly lost seats in the House of Representatives and nearly lost control of it. The idea that they have no place to go is wrong. They can stay home. If this is a long-term trend, it will be very bad news for conservatives.

In the wake of the 1998 election, some religious conservatives began talking openly of opting out of electoral politics altogether. Paul Weyrich, the same man who helped to organize southern ministers for the Republicans in 1980 and was one of the midwives of the Moral Majority, released a remarkable letter on February 19, 1999, in which he stated that politics is a dead end for religious conservatives and that they should concentrate their efforts on the private sphere rather than the public arena.

While "conservatives have learned to succeed in politics" by electing candidates to public office, Weyrich wrote, they failed to enact their agenda because "politics itself has failed." It failed, he went on, "because of the collapse of the culture. The culture we are living in becomes an ever-wider sewer. . . . I think we are caught up in a cultural collapse of historic proportions, a collapse so great that it simply overwhelms politics."

On one level Weyrich feels that the Republican leadership has failed to transform the nation. He has felt strongly that way for a long time, and he never had much confidence in Newt Gingrich as Speaker of the House. But beyond that, he feels that his side has lost the culture war, a judgment for which there is considerable backing and was declared as long ago as 1992 by the neoconservative wise man Irving Kristol. Weyrich was appalled by the unprecedented high approval rating for President Clinton even after the impeachment trial. "If there were really a moral majority out there," he said, "Bill Clinton would have been driven out of office months ago."

I think the level of public support for the president may be illusory, but Weyrich really believes that the battle must be fought on the cultural level rather than the political level right now. "I know that what we have been doing for 30 years hasn't worked," he concluded, "that while we have been fighting and winning in politics, our culture has decayed into something approaching barbarism. We need to take another track, find a different strategy."

Shortly after the stir caused by Weyrich's letter, the advance copies were released of *Blinded by Might: Can the Religious Right Save America?* a book written by two of Falwell's original lieutenants at the Moral Majority: Cal Thomas, who became a nationally syndicated columnist, and Ed Dobson, who became a Baptist pastor in Michigan. To the delight of the liberal media establishment, they went further than Weyrich and said that Christian organization in politics was a mistake. "If the so-called Religious Right focuses mainly on politics to deliver us," they wrote, "we will never get that right because politics and government cannot reach into the soul. That is something that God reserves for himself."

I'm not saying that Paul Weyrich, much less Cal Thomas

and Ed Dobson, can by their leadership extract the religious
foot soldiers from the political trenches. But to the extent
that other cultural conservatives feel as they do, that the political process is closed to them, then that's a warning siren in
the night for Republicans, enhanced by the departure from
the party in 1999 of Bob Smith and Pat Buchanan (a matter
I'll take up at greater length later). Republican leaders have
to convince Weyrich and people like him that the party is
open to their concerns.

So how to do that? First, Republicans cannot give the
impression that they are abandoning the abortion issue. I
may sound as if I'm engaged in realpolitik here because it
sounds as if I am saying they can abandon it but not give the
impression that they are abandoning it.

Be that as it may, the truth is that Ronald Reagan, the
Republican who brought the religious conservatives into the
party, never did very much about abortion. When he was
governor of California, after all, he signed the bill that legal-
ized abortion there. (A great irony of Reagan's presidential
campaign in 1980 was that when his aides decided to run an
ad in New Hampshire to show that Reagan was not just
some movie actor but the former governor of California,
they wanted to depict him signing a bill. But the only available footage of him was his signing of the abortion legalization law, and that became the endlessly repeated Reagan
campaign ad.)

Reagan later said that signing that bill was a mistake and
is fondly remembered by social conservatives as a pro-life
force. When the annual pro-life parade came to Washington
during his years as president, Reagan always met with the
leaders and addressed the anti-abortion forces via a telephone hookup. But he never did much in terms of real policy.

What a candidate cannot do is get out there and say,

"This doesn't matter much to us." That's the impression that Bob Dole gave in 1996 when he said he hadn't read and wouldn't read the party platform reiterating opposition to abortion. That's a little bit of the impression that George W. Bush presented in his early, tentative statements from Austin, even though both Dole and the younger Bush are avowedly pro-life.

But apart from abortion, the larger issue is that Republican leaders have to give the impression that they care about the Christians. They have to indicate that it's not only the right-wing candidates like Pat Buchanan and Gary Bauer who care, but that *all* Republicans care. I don't think anybody has to change positions on the issues, but they do have to change their outlook.

The Republican establishment needs to recognize that the party's strength is in the South. It's a southern party now. The geographical bases of the two parties have shifted dramatically over the past half-century, with the Republican party trading House seats in the Northeast for seats in the South.

Just how much the Republican party has changed can be seen by comparing the makeup of state delegations in the House from the Northeast and from the South in the 80th Congress (1947–1948) and the 104th Congress (1995–1996). These Congresses represented the high-water marks of Republican voting strength in the second half of the twentieth century when on each occasion the GOP seized control of Congress while a Democrat was in the White House.

The strength of the Christian Coalition and of the religious conservatives, moreover, is in the South and the Midwest, where the party needs to remain strong as the population of America moves south and west. Since World War II, the Northeast has lost thirty-six seats, while the

Shifting Party Strength in the Northeast and in the South, 80th and 104th Congresses

	80th Congress (1947–1948)			104th Congress (1995–1996)		
Northeast	R	D	I	R	D	I
Connecticut	6	0	0	3	3	0
Delaware	0	1	0	1	0	0
Maine	3	0	0	1	1	0
Massachusetts	9	5	0	2	8	0
Maryland	2	4	0	4	4	0
New Hampshire	2	0	0	2	0	0
New Jersey	12	2	0	8	5	0
New York	28	16	1	14	17	0
Pennsylvania	28	5	0	10	11	0
Rhode Island	0	2	0	0	2	0
Vermont	1	0	0	0	0	1
West Virginia	4	2	0	0	3	0
Total	**95**	**37**	**1**	**45**	**54**	**1**
South	R	D	I	R	D	I
Alabama	0	9	0	3	4	0
Arkansas	0	7	0	2	2	0
Florida	0	6	0	15	8	0
Georgia	0	10	0	8	3	0
Kentucky	3	6	0	4	2	0
Louisiana	0	8	0	3	4	0
Mississippi	0	7	0	1	4	0
North Carolina	0	12	0	8	4	0
Oklahoma	2	6	0	5	1	0
South Carolina	0	6	0	4	2	0
Tennessee	2	8	0	5	4	0
Texas	0	21	0	11	19	0
Virginia	0	9	0	5	6	0
Total	**7**	**115**	**0**	**74**	**63**	**0**

R = Republican, D = Democratic, I = Independent

South has picked up fifteen seats. The establishment needs to wake up to the fact that the Grand Old Party has a new base with new voters for the twenty-first century. If it is going to control the U.S. government, it will do so with a southern accent.

Stand Firm in Support of the Right to Life

Republican Congressman Jim Courter, a moderate conservative, began the 1989 campaign for governor of New Jersey in what the polls described as a dead heat against his Democratic opponent, Congressman James J. Florio. But the consensus of the political community favored Courter. He was a popular, outgoing personality in the House, marked by colleagues for a political future with no limit. In contrast, Florio was considered moody, abrasive, and sometimes arrogant, and he had lost a race for governor eight years earlier.

Courter's record in Congress had been anti-abortion, but he was not a crusading pro-lifer by any means. Although Florio had once been an ardent foe of abortion, he had followed many other liberal Democrats into the pro-choice camp. Abortion hardly figured to be an issue in the race for governor, but it became exactly that in July of that year, when the U.S. Supreme Court upheld a Missouri law imposing some restrictions on abortion. Florio opposed the ruling; Courter routinely endorsed it.

The wrath of the abortion rights lobby came down on Courter's head, and the polls showed him dropping. Panicking, he reversed himself and pledged that as a governor, he would never interfere with a woman's choice. That provided an opening for Florio, who ran television commercials depicting Courter as Pinocchio, whose nose grew as he told one lie after another. On Election Day, in a state accustomed to razor-thin margins in elections for governor when neither candidate was an incumbent, Florio won in a landslide with 62 percent to Courter's 38 percent.

The abortion rights lobby hailed this result as a signal victory and issued this warning: no pro-life candidate could survive in an urban political battleground state like New Jersey. But another lesson could be drawn from Courter's debacle. He lost not because he was pro-life but because he waffled on abortion (and on gay rights and gun control as well). It was the Pinocchio image that destroyed him.

Indeed, in the decade since Courter's defeat, pro-life Republicans have been able to win races in states similar to New Jersey: Senator Alfonse D'Amato in New York in 1992; Governor John Engler in Michigan in 1990, 1994, and 1998: Governor Robert Taft in Ohio in 1998; Senator Rick Santorum in Pennsylvania in 1994. The lesson for GOP candidates is not to equivocate. To do so is to lose support from friends and foes alike.

• • •

In the 1980s and early 1990s abortion was the red-hot issue for mobilizing conservatives—and for mobilizing liberals too. A lot of presidential elections were fought over abortion, as activists on the left and the right emphasized the president's power to appoint Supreme Court justices. When Ronald Reagan was president, the pro-life movement really felt that abortion could be like the slavery issue had been before the Civil War—a moral crusade whose appeal would grow stronger with each passing year. But what they forgot was that until the Civil War was fought and won, abolitionist sentiment was never endorsed by a majority in the country. Likewise, the desire to eliminate abortion completely through a constitutional amendment has never commanded majority support. A decade after the end of Ronald Reagan's term, abortion has become a less salient issue, and the stakes do not seem as high.

The main reason for the decline of the abortion issue's political power is that moral issues tend to exhaust people over time. Twenty-five years ago, for example, busing to accomplish racial integration in public schools was an enormous emotional issue that inspired riots, demonstrations, political upheavals. A politician could hardly go on *Meet the Press* without being asked his position on busing. But the fires faded. Many white families were able to avoid busing by moving into new neighborhoods or turning to private and parochial schools. It became obvious that busing was not only a blunt instrument but a clearly ineffective one in addressing educational imbalances, and it fell sharply on the civil rights priority list.

Something approaching that process has softened the impact of abortion. The number of abortions has declined, but more significant is the realization by both sides that they cannot achieve their maximum goals. Abortion will not be outlawed, but it will be restricted. This is aided by a conscious but unstated strategy by the Republican party leadership to neutralize the issue. When Haley Barbour was national chairman (1993–1996), he tried to conquer the abortion dilemma by dividing the issue into its component parts. Then he set about identifying which of those elements were popular and could muster majority support. There are three such anti-abortion proposals, all of which fall short of a futile crusade for a human life amendment to the federal Constitution.

Late-term or partial-birth abortions. This involves banning not only third-trimester abortions but also the "partial-birth" procedure—most often practiced in the second trimester—described in the federal legislation as an operation "in which the person performing the abortion partially vaginally delivers a living fetus before killing the fetus and completing the delivery." All but the most radical abortion-rights advocates support a ban on late-term abortions. Senator Daniel Patrick Moynihan of New York, who like most other mainstream Democrats drifted into the pro-choice camp after the 1973 *Roe v. Wade* decision, called the process "the next thing to infanticide" and voted to override President Clinton's 1998 veto of a ban on partial-birth abortions. So did the nominally pro-choice Democratic leaders of the House and Senate, though the veto was sustained.

Federal funding. The various Hyde amendments (sponsored by the doughty pro-life advocate, Representative Henry Hyde of Illinois) barred federal spending for abortions as part of welfare programs, in military hospitals, and in the District of Columbia. Because these amendments were attached to appropriations bills, they constituted the only anti-abortion measures that were able to escape Clinton's veto.

Parental consent or notification. The requirement of consent by one or both parents before an abortion can be performed had been passed by eleven states by the summer of 1999, though three were under court challenge. The less stringent requirement that one or both parents must be notified had been passed in an additional twenty-three states, with seven under court challenge. In 1999, Governor George W. Bush pushed through to passage a notification bill in Texas, and in New Jersey, Republican Governor Christine Todd Whitman signed a parental notification bill, even though she had vetoed a partial-birth abortion ban two years earlier, incurring the wrath of pro-lifers.

Haley Barbour hoped to use these tactics to chip away at abortion without mounting a frontal assault, and he did succeed in seizing the initiative from the abortion rights lobby while offering some proposals that most Republicans in Congress and state legislatures could agree on.

A side effect has been to provide an escape hatch for pro-choice Republicans. Senator Paul Coverdell of Georgia, Senator Kay Bailey Hutchison of Texas, and Governor Tom Ridge of Pennsylvania are all pro-choice, but they all support the half-measures in the Barbour plan (which are opposed by the National Abortion Rights Action League and its most faithful Democratic supporters, such as Senator Ted Kennedy). The practical outcome has been to give a kind of respectability to the Republican pro-choicers, but ends up fully satisfying no one. The anti-abortion movement's efforts are diluted, and the rich, influential Republicans who are on the other side remain upset that abortion is an issue at all.

Jeffrey Bell, a veteran Republican and pro-life activist, has long predicted that the GOP would become "operationally pro-choice." That is an exaggeration, I believe, but it remains true that in 1999, the leading Republican candidates all seemed to have written off any possibility of barring abortions through a constitutional amendment.

• • •

The Republican party is coming to a crisis in 2000 on this issue, and a lot rides on how it chooses to handle it. The fight is likely going to revolve around the choice of a vice-presidential running mate, since all of the presidential contenders are pro-life. (In 1996, Senator Arlen Specter of Pennsylvania and Governor Pete Wilson of California were the only pro-choice candidates, and both dropped out early.)

The pressure on party leaders to name a pro-choice running mate will be felt not only from the country club women, but also from the Team 100 people who give money and say, "We've got to do something about this."

A classic case of this syndrome was the experience of Senator John McCain of Arizona as he began his campaign for the 2000 Republican presidential nomination.

In mid-February 1999, McCain addressed a private fund-raising dinner in the San Francisco Bay area attended almost entirely by the high-tech entrepreneurs of Silicon Valley. As chairman of the Senate Commerce Committee, McCain had direct jurisdiction over legislation that was vital to their companies. Consequently, they might have been expected to bombard him with questions about computers, telecommunications and the Internet. They didn't. Instead, the nearly all-male audience peppered McCain with questions about abortion. What would he do to a woman's right to choose? Would he press to overturn the Supreme Court's *Roe v. Wade* decision? What would happen to women if that happened? One of these high-powered executives quoted his wife's concern, but many others probably were influenced by their spouses as well.

McCain was a typical Republican senator in that he voted

a straight anti-abortion line on legislation but seldom took the Senate floor to discuss the subject and, in truth, really did not know much about it. Battered by the questions, McCain looked shattered. That may explain his behavior some six months later when he returned to the Bay area. Meeting with the *San Francisco Chronicle*'s editorial board, the Senator declared: "Certainly in the short term, or even the long term, I would not support repeal of *Roe v. Wade*." Anti-abortion forces reacted in rage. Gradually, McCain peeled back until five days later, he wrote the National Right to Life Committee affirming that—yes, definitely, and no ands, buts or ifs—he wanted to overturn *Roe v. Wade*.

The incident reflects three uncomfortable facts of life inside the GOP. First, candidates seeking money can expect emotional, intense pro-choice sentiment from their principal sources of funding. Second, any obeisance to this sentiment will produce an emotional adverse response from pro-life elements that are important to the party's success. Third, nearly all the candidates give little thought to abortion and are helplessly inept in dealing with this crossfire. It is not a happy situation for the Republican party.

As a result, Barbour and other strategists have begun saying publicly that it is time for the party at least to consider a pro-choice Republican on the ticket. They think they can have it both ways: endorse a platform that is against partial-birth abortion, against federal funding, for parental notification, and perhaps still give lip-service to at least the concept of a human life amendment; so, even if the vice president is pro-choice, the Republicans think they will still present an acceptable face to the pro-life contingent—a doubtful premise.

On the other side, the Democratic party has moved very

fast, even since 1992. As that year's presidential campaign began, both Bill Clinton and Al Gore affected some vestigial pro-life aspects. Clinton had been sort of pro-life as governor of Arkansas, and Gore was very pro-life in Congress. Gore was almost an extreme pro-life politician early in his career, cosponsoring tough anti-abortion legislation with Republican Representative Mark Siljander of Michigan, a Christian conservative.

But as the 1992 campaign began, it became clear that any pro-life tendency by Clinton and Gore was strictly a thing of the past. Any Democratic national ticket is certain to be inflexibly pro-choice, giving voters who are pro-life little real alternative but to support the GOP, especially if the Republican party is sympathetic to the rest of the Christian agenda—as in the case of Senators Coverdell and Hutchison.

There is a real irony in our political culture about abortion. An ordinary person who feels strongly about abortion one way or another usually does not waffle. But politicians tend not to be like ordinary people. Most ordinary people really don't reverse their passionate beliefs that much. But for politicians, there is a tremendous record of shifting strong positions, by Republicans and Democrats alike.

On the one side, both Ronald Reagan and George Bush, Sr., changed their position from pro-choice to pro-life. As I mentioned before, Reagan signed an abortion legalization bill when he was the governor of California prior to taking up the pro-life standard. Bush's switch was blatantly political, taking place when he discovered that not being a pro-life candidate in the Republican primaries can be very difficult.

In 1979 I was traveling with Bush on an early trip to New Hampshire, and he was being hounded by pro-life demonstrators. He was not taken seriously as a contender by anyone at that time (less than 1 percent in the polls), and I was the only journalist traveling with him. He said, almost to himself, "How do I get rid of these people? Are these people going to follow me around all year?" I said, "I'll bet they do, George." And when he responded, "How do I get rid of them?" I told him, "Change your position." He did. I'm certainly not saying that my advice did it, and I never thought he would take me seriously. But he wanted to be president, and that was what the party activists required of him.

On the Democratic side, there have been tremendous changes as well, with Al Gore being the most recent of them. Ted Kennedy was once anti-abortion, as were almost all other Catholic politicians. Jim Florio, the former governor of New Jersey, was fervently pro-life when he was a young congressman and was listed by the speakers' bureau of the National Right to Life Committee, available for anti-abortion speeches around the country. But he switched sides. Jesse Jackson also changed from pro-life to pro-choice.

So the parties are really polarized on abortion, and the Republicans are dangerously polarized within their own ranks—more so than the Democrats. If you read the op-ed pages or listen to the commentators on television, you hear a lot about a revolt at polling places from the country club women and the Team 100 donors, who claim that the pro-life position defeated Bush in 1992 and defeated Dole in 1996, but there is absolutely no evidence to confirm that. Bush and Dole lost on their own merits, for reasons having nothing to do with their position on abortion.

The American electorate tends to divide 40-20-40 in most elections; 40 percent on each side have made their minds up, and there are 20 percent in the middle who can be swayed one way or the other. The Republican pro-choice argument is that these swing voters accept abortion and will be turned off by a pro-life candidate, but the reality doesn't bear this out. The people in the middle simply do not cast their votes on the basis of abortion.

Voters who say, "I'm going to vote this way because of abortion," are generally not in the middle 20 percent, but in the 40 percent who have already made up their mind. What does a person in the middle say? The person in the middle says, "I really don't like abortion, but I don't think you should interfere with a woman's right to choose." That is essentially the consensus in America. That doesn't mean we can have abortions beyond the first trimester. It doesn't mean we can have partial-birth abortions. It doesn't mean a young woman can have an abortion without telling her parents. And it doesn't mean the government should pay for the abortion.

Of the ten people on Governor George W. Bush's presidential exploratory committee, four were pro-choice and six were pro-life—about the breakdown of the Republican party at large. I don't know if this breakdown was an accident, but it seems very calculated to me—a way for Bush to be all things to all people.

However, it hides the real question of whether there will be a revolt by the pro-life people. They're not worried so much because of George W. Bush himself; he's probably more solidly and more sincerely anti-abortion than his father and Bob Dole were on the issue. (In 1999, California abortion rights advocates, perhaps with some exaggeration, designated him as the most anti-abortion governor in America.) But if he takes someone like Pennsylvania Governor Tom Ridge as his vice president, then the fireworks would really start.

Ridge is an interesting fellow: very popular, attractive, relatively conservative, and term limited after his 1998 re-election as governor. An Ivy Leaguer, he was also the first noncommissioned officer/enlisted man combat veteran of the Vietnam War to serve in the House of Representatives. But his stand on abortion poses a serious problem. He is a Roman Catholic, and his hard-nosed local bishop has come very close to reading him out of the church (though he did not excommunicate him from his bishopric as he had the authority to do). Bishop Donald Trautman of Erie, Pennsylvania, requested that Governor Ridge neither speak to nor attend any Catholic functions in his diocese, though he can still take Holy Communion; Ridge accepted the sanction and the authority of his bishop, but did not change his views on abortion.

That's pretty rough stuff—even harsher than what happened in New York in the 1980s between John Cardinal O'Connor and Democratic Governor Mario Cuomo. For all of the heated rhetoric, O'Connor never barred Cuomo from speaking to Catholic groups, though he did challenge the governor's claim to a moral stand. Ridge would not go down easily with a lot of groups, not just Catholics, if tapped for the vice-presidential nomination. In mid-1999, Bush was told by an adviser that a prominent Catholic archbishop (not from Pennsylvania) had informed him that Ridge's being a Catholic makes him less—far less—acceptable on the ticket to active Catholics than a pro-choice Protestant.

It will not do the Republicans' electoral chances any good if they antagonize the religious conservatives into some sort of revolt against a candidate who wants to bring pro-choicers into his inner circle or onto the ticket. We must not forget that the Christian conservatives are the Republicans' foot soldiers, and if they stay home, there is no one to take their place. The logical way to handle this, in my opinion, is to continue to pass the anti-abortion platform and to keep the GOP the anti-abortion party, even though that would make it very difficult—perhaps impossible—to take a vice president who is pro-choice.

It therefore falls to the Republicans to continue the Haley Barbour strategy of separating out the aspects of the abortion issue that have wide support—but to do so within the context of a pro-life party, a party that can make sure the solid Republican voters come to the polls and work to get out the vote.

That's the way Republicans have handled it since 1980, and it worked for a strong candidate like Ronald Reagan. With another strong candidate, it could work just as well in 2000.

Reach Out to Women and Minorities Without Compromising the Message

Throughout the 1990s, moderate Republicans were wringing their hands over the gender gap and the race gap—the fact that women and minorities vote heavily Democratic, digging a hole for Republican candidates to climb out of. Their solution, of course, was to tailor the Republican message to appeal to these groups—in other words, to become more like the Democrats. I attended a meeting of conservative journalists in the spring of 1999 that discussed at length how the Republicans could offer an effective government proposal for child care.

That is the wrong way to go. The GOP's prospects are dim if it plans to battle the Democrats on issues like child care. If the basic Republican message is a strong one (and I think it is, no matter what the polls say), then there must be a way to appeal to these voters without compromising that message.

Contrary to the conventional wisdom, the gender gap is not essentially an abortion-related problem, although feminists claim that to be the case. It is in much greater part a result of the vulnerability in today's world of unmarried women or women with less than stable home lives. There is a feeling among this group that the Republican party would take care of them less well than the Democratic party would.

The supply-side pioneer Jude Wanniski has a formulation he likes to use: the Democratic party is the "Mommy party" and the Republican party is the "Daddy party"—one is the caring mother and the other the stern father. I think that for this reason, a lot of younger, less educated, lower-income women have become the bedrock of Democratic strength.

But I think the gender gap is a less than permanent feature of the political scene. The fact that George W. Bush ran so well in Texas among women in 1998, capturing a stunning 65 percent of their vote, shows that the discrepancies between male and female voters are not carved in stone. Women respond as well as men do to the Republican vision of liberty and freedom, *if* the issues are presented skillfully. The gender gap is something that very strong candidates can overcome.

Women in the late 1990s were breaking into the leadership of the GOP, particularly in the House of Representatives. Representative Jennifer Dunn of Washington, for example, was a serious (though unsuccessful) candidate for majority leader in 1998. And yet that is unlikely to exert any influence on the gender gap. A woman on the Republican national ticket as the presidential or vice-presidential nominee might be another matter. In the early stages of the 2000 race, Elizabeth Dole, the former cabinet member and president of the American Red Cross, was a serious candidate for president and remained a possibility for vice president.

The Hispanic vote is a more complicated case, because until the late 1990s, the Republicans thought they had a very good chance to lock up this ethnic group. Hispanics in many places are upward achievers, family oriented and success oriented. The big Cuban community in Florida, in particular, is heavily Republican, though that is a special case considering the greater Republican opposition to Fidel Castro. Still, the Mexican-Americans in California, Texas, and elsewhere seemed ripe to be proselytized by the GOP.

But all those prospects diminished radically starting in 1994, after the adoption of California's Proposition 187. Under Governor Pete Wilson, the state's GOP took an exceptionally hard line on immigration, and this has been extraordinarily damaging for the party in a state where whites were fast becoming a minority. The Mexican Americans felt there was real hostility to them within the GOP, and this sense has trickled down to other states and other Hispanic groups as well. Dan Lungren, once thought of as Republican presidential timber, won only 17 percent of the Hispanic vote in his disastrous 1998 campaign for governor (compared with 27 percent for Wilson in his 1994 reelection, a level that was considered disappointing at the time).

On the other hand, in Florida and Texas, two of the other states with large Hispanic populations, the Bush brothers did very well with the Hispanic vote in 1998, at the same time that Lungren was sinking. Jeb Bush speaks fluent Spanish and is a converted Catholic, married to a naturalized Mexican. George W. Bush speaks pretty good Spanish and has also made inroads into the Hispanic vote. Jeb's 61 percent and George W.'s 49 percent shares were not matched by other Republicans. In New York, Republican Governor George Pataki won an easy reelection against a weak Democratic opponent but managed to win the vote of only 25 percent of the Hispanics. Still, the Bush performance was a cause for optimism, showing that this big and growing ethnic group was attainable for a Republican candidate.

The black vote is the toughest of all. The situation here

has been getting worse and worse with each year: the hostility toward Republicans, the feeling that Republicans don't give a damn about black people, is pervasive. It is here that the Republicans have the most work to do.

The Republicans' difficulties with blacks started in 1960 when John F. Kennedy made a big pitch for the black vote. The mythology is that the tide was turned when he made a well-publicized telephone call to Martin Luther King's wife, when the civil rights leader was put in jail, but the simple fact is that he was much more appealing than his Republican opponent, Richard M. Nixon, to blacks—as indeed he was to other ethnic groups—based on personality as much as anything else.

I can say this with confidence because I was a reporter for *The Wall Street Journal* at that time, and I conducted street-corner interviews in Harlem, on Chicago's South Side, and in Baltimore's inner city, as part of a nationwide survey of the African American vote and wrote the article about its results. We found massive support for Kennedy against Nixon. Significantly, the survey was taken before the famous King telephone call. Kennedy already had the black vote locked up.

It's not that Nixon didn't try. Nixon had Jackie Robinson working for him and campaigned hard in New York City with the baseball great at his side. But it wasn't all Nixon's fault. It was just becoming clear that the cards were stacked against the GOP on the black vote, that African Americans truly had turned Abraham Lincoln's picture to the wall. Since the coming of the New Deal, Democratic welfare programs had made the difference. The slight improvement in the black presidential vote for Dwight D. Eisenhower in 1952 and 1956 reflected the breadth of his popularity as a war leader and the lack of appeal of his elitist Democratic opponent, Adlai E. Stevenson.

In 1964 and 1968, Barry Goldwater and Richard Nixon appealed more directly to the disaffected white voters opposed to Lyndon Johnson's social welfare and civil rights policies, and this hammered the nail in the coffin for the Republicans with the black vote. Blacks, after all, were great beneficiaries of LBJ's Great Society and now came to see the GOP as their enemy.

Since then, the Republican share of the black vote in presidential elections has fallen to about 5 to 8 percent for the Republican candidate in each election. In 1996, Bob Dole chose Jack Kemp as his running mate, in part because there was no nationally known Republican who was stronger for working in the black community and going into black neighborhoods. But Dole didn't do any better among black voters than Bush had done four years before. In fact, Kemp was criticized by his fellow Republicans for spending too much time campaigning in the inner city.

A parallel development is that the Republicans have become the southern party, and blacks are keenly aware of the history of the South. Since 1994, when the Republicans regained control of Congress, the political leadership has come mostly from states like Georgia, Texas, Mississippi, Louisiana, and Oklahoma, all former Confederate states or territories. In 1999, only the Speaker, Dennis Hastert of Illinois, was from the North, and he ascended only after two southerners—Newt Gingrich of Georgia and Bob Livingston of Louisiana—had bowed out.

The journalist Christopher Caldwell wrote an article in *The Atlantic Monthly* in 1998 titled "The Southern Captivity of the Republican Party," in which he declared that

"Southerners now wag the Republican dog." He contended that "Democratic excesses since the '70s may have destabilized the Republican Party by chasing [southern conservatives] into the fold." Caldwell argues that this turned the GOP "into a machine that is steadily becoming too conservative for the country." I disagree, but he is absolutely correct that the fact that the party of Lincoln speaks with a southern accent is an overriding change that at the very least makes a quest for the black vote difficult indeed.

To get an idea of what the Republican party faces, it is instructive to look at the North Carolina results from 1998, when Senator Lauch Faircloth was defeated by John Edwards, a handsome, flamboyant, articulate and very rich Democratic trial lawyer. Faircloth was kind of a good ol' boy—little education, not very articulate. He got beaten heavily, winning only 57 percent of the white vote and 6 percent of the black vote. In the South in the 1990s, a Republican had to get at least 70 percent of the white vote to win because the party got so little of the black vote.

This racial divide thus feeds on itself. The way to win, most Republican strategists say, is to maximize white support, not to dribble it away trying fruitlessly to get black support. And so the risk for the party is that if it cannot hold onto that 70 percent of the white vote, it may well lose its base in the South.

The two most interesting Democratic victories in the Deep South in the previous two elections were Mary Landrieu's victory in the 1996 Senate race in Louisiana and the election of Jim Hodges as governor of South Carolina in 1998. Both campaigns were fueled by gambling interests, which spent a lot of money turning out the black vote in very high percentages. In each race, the Republican candidate's opposition to gambling unwittingly generated a campaign that maximized the African American vote.

So, if the Democrats retain such a lock over the entire black vote, the Republicans run the risk of losing many seats that they ought to win. Even black Republican candidates have fared no better with black voters. A classic example came in Michigan over a decade ago. Bill Lucas, an African American former policeman who had been a prodigious Democratic vote getter in Wayne County (Detroit) as sheriff and county executive, had switched to the Republican party and was the GOP candidate for governor in 1986. He managed to get only 23 percent of the black vote while attracting far fewer whites (30 percent) than the typical Republican statewide candidates. Other black Republican candidates have fared little better with African American voters. Alan Keyes, a former high diplomatic official in the Reagan administration with a Ph.D. from Harvard, captured no more than 10 percent of African American voters in his two races for the Senate from Maryland in 1988 and 1992.

But all is not lost for the Republicans; they just have to adjust their way of thinking. Even though most Republicans are unable even to make a dent in the black vote, some have been able to get a good chunk of it: George W. Bush in Texas, former New Jersey Governor Tom Kean, and current New Jersey Governor Christine Todd Whitman, to name just a few. A very strong Republican candidate with blacks, surprisingly, was the conservative Governor John Engler of Michigan, who won 27 percent in his 1998 reelection run. George W. Bush also collected 27 percent in Texas that year. And significantly, neither Engler nor Bush was a liberal Republican in the Kean-Whitman mold.

What these candidates have in common is they are not

threatening to blacks, they do not present themselves as old-fashioned southern whites, and they make a point to go to the black neighborhoods. I traveled with George W. Bush in one black neighborhood in San Antonio during the 1998 campaign. He had brought down from Austin a black state official whom he had appointed. Bush was approachable and was at ease. I have seen a lot of Republicans campaigning in black neighborhoods who seemed terribly uncomfortable and out of touch. That was not the case for Governor Bush. But such examples are regrettably rare.

The second thing that these candidates have learned is that in addition to trying very, very hard, they must also maintain low expectations. Most politicians have difficulty coming to grips with not winning outright in every community. What too many Republicans fail to realize is that in the black community, all they need to do is get 20 to 25 percent of this vote—or even less. They think of 20 percent as still losing and not worth pursuing. They don't realize that, particularly in the South, where there is a sizable black vote, much bigger than in the North, even 20 percent can mean the difference between winning and losing, especially if it's getting harder and harder to get 70 percent of the white vote.

But let's be honest: the black vote is very frozen. I'm just talking about chipping away little parts of it because a little bit can mean a lot. The important thing the Republicans have to do is to avoid the things that really look as if they are hostile to these nonwhite voters. For example, for thirty years, the GOP has made a big issue out of ballot security and voting booth security, which tends to focus mostly on the integrity of the vote in minority neighborhoods. (In 1968, with the help of Republican poll watchers, I wrote a column that got a lot of attention about votes being stolen in

Chicago's inner-city precincts, but it surely was not a love letter to African American citizens.) Right or wrong, this comes across as an attempt to intimidate the black vote. Whatever the Republicans find in fraudulent votes is more than compensated by the push this effort gives to the Democrats, who portray it as a return to the segregated South and stressed this attack in 1998.

This is the equivalent of what happened to California's Hispanic vote with the anti-immigration proposals (and also claims of vote stealing), which gained the Republicans nothing and lost them a lot, not only there but also in key states like Illinois, New York, and New Jersey. If the Republicans keep slicing off pieces of the electorate, soon they're going to find themselves with a very small target.

• • •

Complicating the situation is the lingering issue of affirmative action or (as it is more accurately described) racial quotas. Two or three years ago, whenever I attended private meetings with Republican congressmen, I found that they were solidly in favor of taking some kind of action on racial quotas. This has almost completely dissipated, not because public opinion has changed but because the Republicans do not want to storm off into battle without a president of their party to lead the charge. This is yet another sign of the Republicans' timidity.

The fact is that abolishing racial quotas remains popular. Wherever it is put before the electorate, this proposition carries in referendums. It carries in the polls. People think that quotas are unfair. They take literally, not figuratively, Martin Luther King's "dream" that his children "will be judged not by the color of their skin but by the content of their character." I think most of these people are sincere and are not racist. They feel deep resentment if they or their children don't get into college, don't get a job, don't get a promotion because they are white. They feel that there should not be any racial discrimination against whites or blacks, that the process should be evened up.

Now, granted, this sentiment is mostly limited to non-black Americans. But there is a principle involved, and the Republicans have allowed themselves to be frightened away from sticking to it. Newt Gingrich lost all stomach for the fight when Congressman John Lewis—a fellow Georgian and a notable African American civil rights leader in the 1960s—rose up against him on this issue. Gingrich then began to doubt himself and often raised the point of how he could make this fight on affirmative action if it was against the inclination of John Lewis (who, incidentally, was merciless in chastising Gingrich on every conceivable issue, including the Speaker's ethics and had compared him to Hitler). At a 1995 dinner for mostly conservative journalists, the speaker railed at me for criticizing his position on racial quotas, invoking the heroism of Lewis.

Even more daunting for Republicans is the position taken by Representative J. C. Watts, one of Gingrich's protégés who, after the 1998 elections, defeated John Boehner to be elected chairman of the House Republican Conference. The only African American Republican in Congress, Watts announced his opposition to changing the law on racial quotas as it now stands. He is not a moderate; he is a conservative. It is almost a measure of where the Republicans are that they do not want to move on affirmative action if they do not have J. C. Watts with them. Don't forget: Watts represents an Oklahoma constituency that is 93 percent white, so he could do anything he wants on this issue. But he feels that it is his duty, as a black man, not to assail the structure of affirmative action.

That gives lots of Republicans pause. If they have only one member of their entire congressional caucus who is African American and he is saying that he's not going to stand with them, it's a killer.

Then you have Ward Connerly, the Sacramento black businessman and University of California regent who successfully championed the anti-quota Proposition 209 in 1996 in California and pushed to victory a similar referendum in the state of Washington in 1998. Connerly went to Florida in 1999 to run the campaign there for a similar referendum and had a meeting with Jeb Bush, the new governor. To Connerly's astonishment, Bush trashed him, telling reporters, "He wants a war. I'm a lover." Connerly was taken aback. He had to run his campaign with the Republican governor opposed to him.

That is now the conventional wisdom: the Republicans don't even borrow the Clinton line of "mend it, don't end it"; they just want the issue to go away. And this at a time when public opinion has been so overwhelmingly anti-quota that there was at least a possibility that the American people would consider ending it rather than mending it.

In 1992, Democrats were deathly afraid of the issue, realizing that quotas were necessary for their black constituency but poison for the rest of the electorate. During that year's presidential primary campaign in New York, I attended a *New York Post* editorial board meeting with candidate Bill Clinton. As a guest, I was given one question to ask, and I asked Clinton whether he would terminate the quota system inside the federal government. "Oh," Clinton replied, brushing me off. "You're not going to get me on that." At that point, it seemed that even mending the system might be suicidal politically.

Seven years later, in 1999, the Republicans were so afraid, as Jeb Bush said, of being tarred as "haters" if they endorse repealing affirmative action that they were paralyzed. But I think that if the issue is posed correctly, it might actually help the Republicans with certain black voters. Certainly I don't think it could make things any worse and would not seriously impede an effort to bring over blacks.

One of the problems is using the words *affirmative action*. That displays the Republican ineptitude in dealing with issues. Steve Horn, a moderate Republican congressman from California, who is the former president of Long Beach State University, has tried very hard to try to get the words *affirmative action* out of Republican rhetoric and to say instead that the party is against racial quotas. The Republicans, with their typical lack of discipline and tactical vigor, have slipped back into using the Democratic term.

The reason that this language distinction is an important point is that the two terms mean different things. *Affirmative action* is a state of mind; *racial quotas* are hard and fast numerical requirements. It is at least theoretically possible under affirmative action to say, "We need blacks in here, but we're not going to establish quotas and we're not going to have prejudicial decisions." The Republicans can support outreach without abandoning their principles. The Republicans believe in the free market, after all, and so do a lot of voters—of all racial backgrounds. If they're going to get around the conflict with black voters over this issue, they need to reframe it as one of freedom and fairness. That's where the Republicans could use it.

Republicans can reach out to new voters by saying that the free economic system is to the benefit of everybody, blacks and whites alike. Remember that the Republicans are not trying to get 70 percent, or 60 percent, or 50 percent, or even 40 percent of the black vote; they need to think about getting 20 or 25 percent. And they can get 20 percent with this approach.

I also think it's important for race relations in the country. Racial quotas are truly destructive of our system—destructive of whites and destructive of blacks. They stir up more bad feelings than good. Racial quotas lead to racial hostility, racial animosity, resentment. So you find in big universities resentment by some of the whites that the blacks are there, and resentment by the blacks that they are a special category, and that leads to more segregation.

There is nearly total silence on the issue. Ward Connerly is nearly a voice in the wilderness, but he does get the votes. I don't believe that wholly on the basis of racial prejudice or anti-black feeling, you could get these kinds of votes in the states of California or Washington.

If a Republican presidential candidate were to speak in these terms, rather than playing on white resentment, he could take this discussion to a whole new level and even win over some black votes, which is more than the party is doing now. Ward Connerly, as an African American, does speak in those terms. Other Republicans can too.

Endorse a Foreign Policy Based on Strength and Engagement, But for the Right Reasons

The U.S. military intervention in Kosovo in the spring of 1999 revealed a tremendous split within the Republican party. On one side were those who felt that this was an overreach of power—something that the United States should not have been doing and that the Republican party should not have been sanctioning. The others took the position that this was a chance for the Republicans to be even more aggressive than Bill Clinton in foreign policy and even more interventionist.

Most Republicans in Congress took the first position, declining to support the president's policy and dealing him embarrassing setbacks like the vote in Congress on April 28, 1999, when the House chose not to endorse the bombing campaign against Yugoslavia. The specific vote on bombing was 213 to 213, the first time in memory that a U.S. military operation was not endorsed by Congress. The party leadership's position was muffled here with Speaker Dennis Hastert passively supporting and voting for the bombing but Majority Whip Tom DeLay, technically third in command but perhaps the most powerful Republican in the House, actively opposing it.

On the other side, the leading Republican interventionist

voices were those of Arizona Senator John McCain, who was himself running for president, and conservative commentator and strategist William Kristol, editor and publisher of *The Weekly Standard.*

From the start of NATO's hostilities against Yugoslavia, McCain insisted on winning the war. In contrast to other Republican presidential candidates, he advocated the deployment and use of ground troops to invade Kosovo to restore the ethnic Albanian population to their homes. McCain, the son and grandson of admirals, is a navy aviator who had been shot down over North Vietnam and held prisoner for nearly six miserable years. He was more hawkish than Clinton or his fellow Republican presidential candidates, among whom only Elizabeth Dole later eased into overtly supporting the Kosovo invasion option.

Bill Kristol is a more interesting case. For several years leading up to the Kosovo war, he had been looking for a foreign policy issue to champion, on the belief that foreign policy is the real Republican issue for 2000. Kristol and a lot of other Republican strategists correctly perceived that the Republicans lost something with the winning of the Cold War, the conduct of which had been a unifying force for most Republicans.

For four decades, across the political spectrum, nearly everyone in the GOP was a Cold Warrior. Not only that, but the global struggle with the Soviet Union was a unifying element between the party and the American people. Before the crisis in Kosovo erupted in the spring of 1999, Kristol had seized on China as the new enemy, a focus around which the Republicans could recreate the Cold War to the immense advantage of the party.

China was not Yugoslavia. A powerful nation still ruled

by an autocratic Communist dictatorship and growing more powerful, it boasted nuclear weapons and was developing the means to deliver them. The allegation of espionage at the nuclear weapons laboratory at Los Alamos, New Mexico, was only the latest manifestation of what was portrayed as the Chinese threat, and Kristol used his platform at *The Weekly Standard* to pound the Clinton administration mercilessly on its accommodationist China policy. Of course, the president was part of the target because of evidence in the campaign finance scandals that China was used as a milk cow for the Democratic campaign of 1996.

But Kristol and his allies ran into a roadblock on the China issue. First, the business community is strong on engagement with China and opening the Chinese market to American firms. Such left-wing critics as my esteemed colleague, commentator-columnist Mark Shields, would say that these executives are just interested in making a buck. In truth, they really do believe that it is senseless to let the Europeans get all of the business out of China, and the diplomats of course feel that engagement is a safer course than operating in a confrontational Cold War mode.

I first perceived that Gary Bauer, who had served as undersecretary of education and White House domestic policy chief during the Reagan administration, harbored presidential ambitions of his own during the summer of 1997 when, under my importuning, he indicated he might actually welcome a Cold War–style face-off with China.

Having said all of this, there is a second fact—other than disinclination to confront Beijing—that has prevented the anti-China crowd from gaining much traction: people really don't care that much about China. In the days when we had air raid warnings and civil defense activities for a threatened

Soviet nuclear strike, people took the Cold War seriously; in the 1990s, they no longer stayed awake nights worrying about the Red Menace much less the Yellow Peril. So it has been very difficult for Kristol or for other anti-China Republicans like Bauer to build up public sentiment in this direction.

Kristol found a new outlet with the war in Kosovo, and he pressed the issue in print and on television, urging the Republicans to support whatever military measures would be necessary to drive Yugoslavian President Slobodan Milosevic from power and restore the Kosovar Albanians to their homes. He and his colleague Robert Kagan ran a series of blistering editorials in *The Weekly Standard,* and he was even stronger on ABC's *This Week with Sam Donaldson and Cokie Roberts,* where he went a step further and attacked his fellow Republicans.

"I think Republicans have been misled by their dislike—not to say hatred—of Bill Clinton," Kristol said on March 28. "I really think the vote on Tuesday night in the Senate [38 to 16] among Republicans against authorizing the bombing in Kosovo and Serbia was a big mistake. I think the Republicans, like Senator McCain and others, who voted to authorize force, are shaping the right future for the party."

Kristol went on to make a revealing comment: "Republicans so dislike Bill Clinton, when they should basically be supporting him, as a criticism they should have of him now is that he is lucky to do too little, not that he's doing too much. I am worried about the Republican party. They so dislike Clinton that they're in danger of becoming knee-jerk neoisolationists."

Now there are several interesting points about this.

One point is that here Kristol is dismissing almost all the

people who think this is the wrong policy, on the grounds that they're blinded by their hatred of Clinton. They are not looking at the policy, they are not looking to substance, they are just looking at him.

Second, he is also saying that any criticism of this intervention is isolationist. In other words, if you don't approve a bombing policy, you're a Buchananite—or worse.

Third, he is saying that the Republican litmus test—and here he is in agreement with *The Wall Street Journal*—is how each presidential candidate stands on this issue. In other words, McCain may be unacceptable to many Republicans because of his views on other things (specifically, campaign finance reform and taxing tobacco), but that is to be subsumed by this greater issue.

Fourth, Kristol omits the fact that *The Weekly Standard* has been battering Clinton since the magazine's inception in 1995 (and even a lot of conservatives thought they were going much too far in doing it), which raises a question that he didn't really answer: Have the relentless attacks on Clinton over the past six years reduced his ability as president to lead the nation into war?

The fifth point—the biggest point—follows from Kristol's previous attempt to make China the cutting issue for the Republican party: his view that foreign policy is the best issue for the party. By trumpeting international issues, Kristol implicitly adopts a kind of defeatist attitude toward the Republican domestic agenda of reducing government, reducing taxes, and freedom of the individual. Kristol is saying that these are not popular issues and Republicans cannot win on these issues; therefore, we should promote a bombing policy. Just as Clinton has used bombings (particularly against Iraq) to distract Americans from unpleasant domestic scandals, was not Kristol using the same tactic to distract voters from what he considers an unpleasant Republican agenda?

What's ironic about this development is that in 1993 and 1994, when Kristol was running the Project for the Republican Future, he was the moving force in getting the Republicans to take an aggressive policy against health care reform. At that time, the conventional wisdom by Bob Dole, and even Newt Gingrich up to a point, was that the Republicans could not afford to go into the 1994 election without having passed a health care bill. Kristol changed all that. He said, "Hey, make my day. Attack me for killing that bill." He famously sent out a fax to all the Republican activists and members of Congress, urging them to argue that there was, in fact, no health care crisis. Back then he believed in a strong GOP domestic agenda, and he carried the day.

Now he has become more like Dwight D. Eisenhower in 1952. Eisenhower ran for president for reasons having almost nothing to do with domestic policy. He thought that after twenty years out of power, the Republican party was finally going to win in 1952, and he was terrified that Senator Robert Taft would become president and take the United States out of NATO, out of Europe, out of the Marshall Plan, and return to isolation, to the great benefit of the Soviet Union.

So he ran on those issues and won, and he abandoned much of the Republican platform on domestic policy, an approach bearing grim foreboding for the Republican party's future. He entered the White House with no domestic agenda and never truly developed one during eight years. Taft, in contrast, was deeply committed to domestic issues that were then and are now in the Republican mainstream. The people like Bill Kristol, who are saying that the Republican party has to be based on foreign policy, have forgotten this history.

Ronald Reagan, we ought to remember, did not base his victorious 1980 campaign on foreign policy; he ran on disgruntlement with Jimmy Carter on issues across the board. Most of Reagan's campaign speeches were about domestic policy. The idea that Republicans can win only on foreign policy—to repeat—serves primarily to downgrade the entire agenda (what I would call the "freedom agenda": freedom to conduct your business, freedom from government, to use your own money in the way you want) in favor of a muscular foreign policy.

The only thing I can say to Republicans like my friend Bill Kristol, who insist on the primacy of foreign policy in a political campaign, is that unless the actual security of the United States is threatened (which was not the case in Kosovo), the public is not going to respond. There was once a very popular political science textbook by James MacGregor Burns and J. W. Peltason that had an unintentionally hilarious line about public opinion. They wrote that during World War II, public interest in international affairs increased sharply. Hard to argue with that. In time of war, a shooting war, and to a lesser degree a Cold War, of course there is a great deal of interest in foreign affairs.

There is not that much interest in foreign affairs at other times, and therefore the whole idea that Republicans are at an advantage here, and should stress this, is nonsensical politically. With the advent of the volunteer armed forces (a Republican invention, by the way), Johnny and Sally are not going to go marching off to fight or occupy the Balkans unless they want to. That distances the ordinary American from the implications of foreign policy in a way that was not possible during the days of military conscription.

The split over Kosovo showed a badly divided party, with a majority opposing the McCain-Kristol hawkishness. After Milosevic's capitulation to U.S.-NATO bombing, Kristol and Kagan praised Clinton and censured the Republicans who opposed him. But in terms of supporting foreign intervention, I have never found a strong public commitment for these ventures: the occupation of Haiti, the permanent peacekeeping in Bosnia, the ill-fated mission to Somalia. The apparent inconsistencies also bother a lot of people. Why didn't we send troops to Burundi and Rwanda? Why didn't we ever deal with the Azerbaijan-Armenia war? Why don't we deal with some of the more than fifty wars taking place around the world?

The rule of thumb is that we intervene where there are television cameras, and we don't intervene where there are no television cameras. A conflict has to be on television to justify an intervention because the pictures evoke an emotional response. In general, though, the American people could not care less, unless American blood is spilled. Absent that, foreign policy is not going to be of great interest.

In the end, national security suffers from what can be called the mental health syndrome. In the late 1950s, mental health was considered a big issue. It always came up high on the polls because voters were asked, "Do you care about mental health?" and what were they going to say—no? So when voters are asked today, "Do you care about national security?" they are going to say, "Sure, I care," but they really don't. And it would be foolish for the Republican party to build a political campaign on such a shaky foundation.

Finally, why was it that an administration and a Democratic party led by baby boomers, most of whom opposed and most of whom did not fight in the Vietnam War, were so ferociously aggressive about Kosovo? Why was it that the left-of-center governments that now control all of Western Europe and North America became such ardent war hawks? Why was it that critics and opponents of President Bush's war against Iraq were in the forefront of President Clinton's war against Serbia?

Because this was the quintessential liberal's war where national interest was not at stake: no oil, no narrow national interest, only humanitarian considerations—and something else. When on May 27, 1999, an international tribunal in The Hague indicted Milosevic and his colleagues for war crimes, it was truly a liberal's dream of international organizations transcending narrow nationalism. At the same time, in an address to the joint session of the Canadian Parliament, the playwright Vaclav Havel, president of the Czech Republic and a hero of the new Europe, declared the nation-state to be dead.

But why should conservatives like John McCain and William Kristol be purveyors of that dream? That is the question to be pondered by the Republicans going into the 2000 elections.

Don't Be Afraid
of Term Limits

In 1994, when the Republicans won control of the House of Representatives for the first time in forty years, one of the most popular items in their Contract with America was term limits. In every poll, term limits had broad support—almost always more than 70 percent approved—a level that reflected widespread dissatisfaction with the Clinton administration, disillusionment with politics in general, and a lingering influence of Ross Perot's 1992 campaign against professional politicians.

There was also the active U.S. Term Limits organization pushing strenuously for candidates who were pledging to support and adhere to term limits, most of whom were Republicans. The movement's biggest victory came in the state of Washington, where the Speaker of the House, Thomas S. Foley, was defeated for reelection to his seat—the first sitting Speaker thrown out of office since 1860. (It didn't help his cause that Foley had sued the people of Washington for passing a referendum in favor of term limits. He won his suit but lost the election.)

The problem is that the Republicans really didn't mean it when they supported term limits in 1994. They were using term limits as a device, and that was made quite clear right after the election when Dick Armey, the new House majority leader, said, "Now that we have elected a Republican House, maybe there is no more need for term limits." He later claimed he was misquoted, but he wasn't. And his cynicism was lethal to the cause of term limits in the 104th Congress.

The drive for term limits wasn't supposed to be about restoring a Republican House, although the only way it would have a chance of being enacted was through a GOP takeover. This cause really was about trying to install citizen-politicians who would pass legislation that was very difficult to pass otherwise—in particular, radical tax reform. If representatives are going to serve only three terms in the House, then lobbyists are likely to be much less effective in getting to them than they would be in influencing a career politician who needs campaign contributions to stay in office.

The Republicans were obviously not interested in this new political climate. As a result, in a very hypocritical fashion, they framed the votes on term limits in the House in 1995 so that a constitutional amendment could not possibly pass, but that everybody on the Republican side could get on the record as voting for some version of term limits. It was not the GOP's finest hour.

What bothers the Republicans on term limits is that they see it as a loser for them politically, both individually and as a party collectively; the cause might be desirable in theory, but its end game was suicidal for the career politicians who filled the party's ranks. The Democrats, for the most part, are very honest about term limits. They don't like them, and they don't mind saying so.

Tom Foley once told me that the professional politicians will be fighting on this issue long after ordinary people have forgotten about it. In other words, it's very important to the politicians—a matter of life and death, of whether they survive. In contrast, the voter who is a salesman or bricklayer may tell a pollster that he favors term limits, but he may not think about the issue again for another three or four years, if ever. A career politician will ponder the evil of term limits every waking hour if it threatens his livelihood. This makes the momentum for term limits hard to sustain. Foley was right.

What made the Speaker a true prophet and stunned the term limits movement was the Supreme Court's five-to-four decision on May 22, 1995, that the Constitution did not permit the terms of members of the House to be reduced by a majority vote of Congress, by state legislation, or by state referenda. Once again, five Supreme Court justices had deciphered invisible ink in the Constitution, this time protecting the rights of career politicians.

This decision was devastating, just devastating. It meant that a constitutional amendment would be required to institute term limits, and the chances were near zero of achieving that by the usual means of getting two-thirds of both houses of Congress and three-fourths of the state legislatures. The alternative method of calling a constitutional convention was no more promising. Term-limits activists sought but did not find an alternative strategy to the state referenda, which they had hoped would sweep through the whole country. When the Supreme Court struck, twenty-three states had limited terms for their members of Congress—all by referendum.

The atrophy of the movement is shown in the fact, as I mentioned earlier, that the man who beat Tom Foley in 1994, George Nethercutt, broke his word in 1999 and announced his candidacy for a fourth House term in 2000 in violation of his pledge to serve only three terms. This infuriated the people at U.S. Term Limits, who mounted a vigorous campaign to defeat Nethercutt for taking their money and then breaking his word.

The rationale for such infidelity is that if everybody is not term limited, then nobody should be. The pledge breaker asks: "Why should I penalize my district by not having a representative with seniority?" The classic case came in the 1999 special election in Louisiana to fill the vacancy caused by the resignation of Speaker designate Bob Livingston. The winner, State Representative David Vitter, took credit for the only term limits for state legislators that were actually self-imposed by a state legislature rather than dictated by a referendum of the voters, as was the case in seventeen other states. But he refused to commit himself to congressional term limits, promising that he would do his best to build up seniority in Washington. To do otherwise, said Vitter, would be to practice "unilateral disarmament."

One of the very few Republicans who truly believes in term limits is Dr. Tom Coburn of Muskogee, Oklahoma. He was elected in 1994 from a very Democratic district that had never before sent a Republican to Congress. An obstetrician and gynecologist by profession, he returned to Muskogee every weekend to deliver babies. A complaint was soon filed by Democrats with the House Ethics Committee that this practice violated House ethics rules.

This is the congressional mind at work. The logic is as follows: If a House member cannot practice law (and most of them are lawyers) under the ethics rules, why should a colleague be able to practice medicine? That one poses natural conflicts of interest and that the other does not eludes this mind-set. Responding to the complaint, Coburn said that if he had to choose between being a member of Congress and delivering babies in Muskogee, he'd deliver babies in Muskogee and resign from office. They didn't take the dare (knowing he meant it), the ethics charges were dropped, and he stayed in Congress. However, he remained true to his term-limits pledge and did not file his candidacy for a fourth term in 2000.

It's going to be very difficult for the Republicans to hold Coburn's district without him, and party leaders are not happy about it. But what they don't realize is that they may well be able to win a lot of other districts if their candidates try to emulate Coburn by pledging to serve only three terms if elected. They have not encouraged such behavior because it is hard for professional politicians to think this way.

The GOP leaders are short-sighted about this; they look only at how it will affect them, not the party. When Newt Gingrich came in to power in 1994, one of the few real permanent reforms he instituted was to impose term limits of six years on committee chairmen. As that deadline neared, some of the old-bull committee chairmen made this threat: "Hey, I'm not coming back here to be a backbencher." If Representative Benjamin Gilman of New York, chairman of the International Relations Committee, would rather quit than step down, his district might prove difficult for the Republicans to hold.

That led the House Republican leadership to say, "This is going to do us in, because the Democrats have no illusions about term limits." In typical congressional style, Speaker Hastert quietly moderated the Gingrich reform by permitting term-limited chairmen to take over the chairmanship of another committee. Accordingly, Representative James Leach, a liberal Republican from Iowa, as soon as he finished his six-year hitch as Banking Committee chairman in 2001, could move to International Relations, replacing Gilman, a job he much preferred. That defeated the rationale for imposing term limits on chairmen. Whoever said you could trust a member of Congress?

Republican leaders fail to see that term limits will help to enact their agenda, even if they are not personally in Congress to see it take effect. The concept of term limits remains popular with ordinary Americans because it embodies the ideal of the citizen legislator, and only the citizen legislator can take the necessary action on spending, on reforms, on taxes, on Social Security, on Medicare, to reduce government. I still believe that term limits, if it is a widely held and widely practiced policy, could be a great boon for the Republicans. But because of the tunnel vision of the professional politicians, it is the hardest reform to enact.

●   ●   ●

Term limits historically constitute an attempt to turn back the clock to the nineteenth century, when the average length of service of a member of the House was four years. But that average disguises the fact that a great many congressional districts had a tradition of one term only. Abraham Lincoln served but one term in the House, from 1847 to 1849. Nobody served more than one term from that rural downstate Illinois district. He wanted to serve a second term, but his supporters said no; he had had his turn, and now it was someone else's turn. (Thus, it may be said, de facto term limits saved Abe Lincoln from being a congressional lifer so that he could save the Union.)

The reason there were so many one-term House members in the nineteenth century was that members did not have the power and the perks they have today. The pay was nothing, and it was a real sacrifice to serve. Most members of Congress lived in boarding houses in Washington. If you look at an old congressional directory from that time, you'll find that many others lived in cramped, single rooms at the Willard Hotel. It was not pleasant at all, and it became quite common for congressmen to serve a couple of years and then go home to their real lives.

One of the problems with the modern House of Representatives is that the size of the constituency has far outstripped the size envisioned by the founding fathers, which was that each congressman should represent around 30,000 constituents (though it had already slipped in the 1st Congress to one member per 60,000 constituents). Donald Devine, a former political science professor at the University of Maryland who was President Reagan's chief of personnel management, had an idea that we ought to return to the original standard of 30,000 constituents per congressman. He ended up with a House of Representatives with nearly 10,000 members, and I convinced him that this was a little excessive, if well intentioned. I thought you could have a House with 2,000 members as opposed to the current 435.

A lot of things would change, particularly if you have the same salary pool as today—that is, the same amount of money paid to 435 members would be paid to 2,000, only it would be divided up so that each House member would get about one-fifth the current salary. That means the current salary of $136,700 would go down to around $27,000. And since we wouldn't want them to starve or go on food stamps, we would return to the nineteenth-century practice that they could earn money any way they wanted; they could practice law, deliver babies, be journalists, and if the public didn't like what they were doing on the side, they had a ready recourse: they could deny their congressman another term.

The implications of such a reform would play right into the Republicans' agenda for smaller government. Congressional sessions would be shorter, and if we kept the same level of staff, too, serving five times as many members, Congress would be a less pleasant perk-filled power proposition.

This was the idea behind the original proposal in former Tennessee Governor Lamar Alexander's 1996 campaign for the Republican presidential nomination to "cut their pay and send them home; cut their pay in half, cut the sessions in half." Unfortunately, he didn't sell it very well and it didn't go over, so he dropped it and did not use it all in his quickly aborted second try for president in 2000.

I do believe that the only way that we are going to get term limits is by making service in Congress a somewhat less attractive job. The interesting thing is that most members of Congress, in my opinion, cannot make that much money in civilian life. When they say it's a sacrifice, I don't believe so. I have occasionally accompanied a congressman to a high school and almost always some kid asks, "How much do you make?" Kids are really honest. The congressman will say $136,700, and there's a gasp! That much money in America is a fortune (and in 1999 the salary was raised again, to $141,300 effective in January 2000). A lot of congressmen don't want to give up such a great job. Would they hang on so dearly if they got only $27,000?

•   •   •

Although voters like term limits and term limits would advance the Republicans' agenda, the GOP seems to have abandoned it as an issue for 2000. That's a mistake, because it remains a good issue. The congressional Republicans are terrified of losing the marginal seats, and so term limits may be tucked away in the platform as something they do nothing to support, like the constitutional amendment to end abortion.

It will take a dedicated presidential candidate—one who would be term limited in office himself, by the way (as are thirty-eight of the fifty governors)—to spearhead this movement. He won't lose anything personally by advocating term limits for members of Congress, and it could turn the tables in several key states.

It's just a matter of whether the presidential candidate is willing to look Trent Lott and Denny Hastert in the eye and say, yes, this is where I'm going to go and what we, as Republicans, should stand for. And if the presidential candidate has behind him an army of congressional candidates willing to take the term-limit pledge and live up to it (unlike many opportunistic Republicans of 1994), the results could be sweeping and overpowering.

But it seems remote at best. What we need is to have a whole succession of Tom Coburns. A proliferation of Tom Coburns. Who knows? Maybe Tom Coburn should run for president.

PART THREE

Toward Victory

The Search for a Savior

Amid the melancholy enveloping Republican leaders and activists following the 1998 election was a return for most of them to the old political convention that the keystone of political power and the ability to enact an agenda is the presidency, not Congress. Tom DeLay may have felt that one could accomplish enough from Capitol Hill, but more eyes were now focused on the other end of Pennsylvania Avenue.

The frustration of dealing with a president as determined and skilled as Bill Clinton had convinced the great majority of Republicans that political survival depended on winning the presidential election of 2000. A third consecutive Democratic presidential victory, Republicans were convinced, would surely end the six years of Republican control of the House and possibly cost them the Senate as well. Still reeling from the disappointment of 1998, GOP strategists saw the political momentum remaining with the Democrats, as it had been in 1992 when the Republicans lost the presidency and both houses of Congress.

The prospective Democratic nominee, Vice President Al Gore, was no Clinton. He lacked the president's charm, audacity, and political ingenuity. But as a scandal-free family man, he also carried less in the way of moral and ethical baggage. He would not be that easy to defeat. At the 1996 Democratic National Convention, Gore—not Clinton—had been clearly the favorite of rank-and-file liberal delegates, who still grumbled that their president had embraced welfare reform.

Over the next two years, the vice president was tireless in solidifying his support within the Democratic party, signing up early the entire establishment and money base. Potential challengers—Jesse Jackson, Representative Richard Gephardt, Senators Bob Kerrey, John Kerry, and Paul Wellstone—were driven out. Only former Senator Bill Bradley was left to oppose Gore (supported by Kerrey and Wellstone). But Bradley turned out to be more than a token. The former Princeton all-American and professional basketball player became a real threat against Gore. He could raise money and through 1999 gradually moved up in the polls in key states. Contradicting his eighteen-year image in the Senate as a centrist, Bradley was running to Gore's left—and making progress there.

Meanwhile, the Republicans yearned for another Ronald Reagan—someone who would be able to unite social and economic conservatives, to bring together the country club and the religious right, to appeal once again to middle-class, nonideological Democrats. A dozen or so Republicans claimed the Reagan mantle. But, paradoxically, within days of the 1998 election, it became apparent that the party had fixed on not another Reagan but, literally, another Bush.

George W. Bush, son of the former president and re-elected in 1998 as governor of Texas by a landslide, suddenly exploded as the overwhelming choice of the party establishment for the 2000 nomination. How could it be that the namesake of the man so widely regarded in Republican circles as initiating the party's decline was now anointed as the GOP's new messiah, as the instrument of its presidential strategy?

• • •

For the past generation, the principal question that Republicans had been asking in selecting their presidential nominees was: Whose turn is it? Like the Rotary Club, it seemed that the party functioned on the principle that if you stuck around long enough, you deserved to be president.

But by no means did the selection of an anointed party favorite always fit the pattern. For the first two-thirds of the twentieth century, the Republican party's presidential nomination was often fiercely contested.

1920: Senator Hiram Johnson, the California progressive, and General Leonard Wood, seen by many as Theodore Roosevelt's natural heir, dominated the primary elections and were the early leaders in delegates to the national convention. But the clique of conservative senators who controlled the nominating process at the time did not like either man, and the Chicago convention deadlocked. At an infamous 11 P.M. meeting at the Blackstone Hotel (which gave rise to the phrase "smoke-filled room"), the bosses tapped a mediocre member of Senate as the party's standard-bearer: Warren Harding, a poker-playing, philandering, small-town newspaper publisher from Marion, Ohio. He defeated the Democratic candidate, Governor James M. Cox of Ohio, in November.

1928: Secretary of Commerce Herbert Hoover, a millionaire engineer from California, was the early favorite, but he was hardly anointed by the party regulars. They disliked and distrusted Hoover as a nonparty man who had never sought elective office before, and indeed had been seriously considered by prominent Democrats in 1920 as Woodrow Wilson's successor. The Republican party bosses tried to stampede the national convention against Hoover but failed, and Hoover went on to an easy victory in the fall over New York Governor Alfred E. Smith.

1940: There was no anointed party regular candidate as two newcomers battled for the nomination: Robert A. Taft, who had been elected to the Senate from Ohio just two years earlier, and Thomas E. Dewey, then merely the district attorney of Manhattan prior to his long tenure as governor of New York. Into that vacuum, Wall Street financiers and mass media barons engineered the late-starting candidacy of public utilities lawyer Wendell Willkie of Indiana (called the "barefoot boy from Wall Street"), a lifelong Democrat who had never before sought public office and who had been an early Roosevelt New Dealer. In the lobby of Philadelphia's Benjamin Franklin Hotel during the convention, Willkie encountered his fellow Hoosier but opponent, the old-guard Republican James Watson, who told him: "Wendell, you know that back home in Indiana it's all right if the town whore joins the church, but they don't let her lead the choir the first night." Even so, Willkie won the nomination, but he lost in the general election to FDR.

1952: For the previous two elections, Governor Dewey had been nominated, even though he was despised by the party's midwestern regulars. By 1952, it was clearly the turn of Bob Taft, now called "Mr. Republican." But the eastern internationalist wing of the party viewed with dismay Taft's opposition to NATO and the Marshall Plan and saw him as a loser. General Dwight D. Eisenhower, a non-Republican who had never voted in an election, entered the race late and caught up with Taft as the party desperately sought to avoid a sixth straight presidential defeat. The general won the day, against Taft and then against the Democratic nominee, Illinois Governor Adlai E. Stevenson.

1964: On December 10, 1962, *The Wall Street Journal* reported that Governor Nelson Rockefeller of New York seemed to have "an unbreakable hammerlock" on the 1964 Republican presidential nomination. At that point, his long-standing marriage had been dissolved without political consequences. But his support evaporated in 1963 with his remarriage to a much younger woman, and a grass-roots southern-based revolt spurred the party to nominate "Mr. Conservative," Senator Barry Goldwater of Arizona, for president. He was defeated in a landslide by President Lyndon Johnson.

1968: Governor George Romney of Michigan, the dynamic auto executive who had entered politics just six years earlier, was the early leader. He stumbled in national politics, switching positions on Vietnam by saying he had been "brainwashed" into supporting the war on a visit to the war zone. Former Vice President Richard M. Nixon quickly became the party's choice after Romney's collapse, and he won the White House over Vice President Hubert Humphrey.

But starting in 1980, in the successive nominations of Ronald Reagan, George Bush, and Robert J. Dole, the party picked the man whose turn had come.

1980: Ronald Reagan, the former governor of California, had fallen only a few delegates short of depriving President Gerald Ford of the nomination in 1976. Four years later, he was the overwhelming favorite of the party establishment. He slipped in the Iowa caucuses, losing to George Bush in a stunning upset, but recovered quickly in the New Hampshire primary, and his nomination was never in doubt from that point forward.

1988: Vice President Bush was even more clearly the anointed choice than Reagan had been eight years earlier. But he too lost in Iowa, to Senator Robert J. Dole, and he too recovered in New Hampshire to coast to the nomination.

1996: Now it was Dole's turn, and the party establishment supported him. He slipped by losing early primaries in New Hampshire, Delaware, and Arizona, but recovered in South Carolina and went on to win the nomination easily.

It was clear that anointment did not guarantee nomination, as witnessed by the early stumbles of Reagan, Bush, and Dole. But the strength of party support had become so significant by the end of the century that the anointed candidate could slip and seem to be a poor candidate—and still prevail.

In 2000, it was nobody's turn. Would that mean an open fight for the nomination? Or would someone be anointed? An open fight could result in a sure winner (Eisenhower) or a sure loser (Goldwater). The anointment route could nominate the salvation of the party (Reagan) or a hopeless candidate (Dole). There was no clear argument in either direction. But it was indisputable going into the 2000 election that Republican insiders were much, much more comfortable with a sure thing than a contested nomination.

• • •

Who were these insiders of 2000? Certainly not the senatorial clique that had tapped the feckless Warren Harding in 1920. Their ranks were more disparate: a few governors, senior members of Congress, state party chairmen, and important local leaders, as well as members of the Team 100 financial donors.

In the wake of the lackluster performance and decisive defeat of Bob Dole in 1996, the profile of what the 2000 nominee should be and should not be was etched in the minds of these insiders:

- The nominee *should not* be an incumbent senator. Only one such Republican, Harding, had been elected in the twentieth century (and his presidency was not to be cherished). Two other Republican senators who were nominated, Goldwater in 1964 and Dole in 1996, were badly beaten in the general election.
- The nominee *should not* come from Washington, D.C., even if not a member of the Senate. As the incumbent vice president, Richard Nixon lost in 1960; as a private citizen living in New York City, he won in 1968. Gerald Ford, the 1976 loser, was a career congressman until his appointment to the vacant vice presidency in 1973. Ronald Reagan, Jimmy Carter, and to a lesser extent Bill Clinton ran successful campaigns as outlanders against Washington.
- The nominee *should* have shown an ability to win elections, preferably in a big state. Party establishmentarians who distrusted Reagan as nothing but a movie actor were reassured that he had twice carried California, comfortably, for governor. True, Dwight D. Eisenhower

had had no electoral experience prior to his 1952 and 1956 landslides for presidency. But as a war hero who led the "crusade in Europe" against Hitler, he was a special case.

- The nominee preferably *should* be a governor or a former governor. The winners of five out of the previous six elections—Jimmy Carter in 1976, Ronald Reagan in 1980 and 1984, and Bill Clinton in 1992 and 1996—fit that description. No matter that they lacked foreign policy experience. "Governor" is a better candidate's title than "Senator."

- The nominee *should* come from the South or California, as had every presidential election winner since 1964. John F. Kennedy of Massachusetts in 1960 was the last candidate from anywhere else to have been elected. The nation's political balance has decisively shifted south and west from the Northeast-Midwest quadrant that dominated for the first sixty years of the century.

- The nominee *should* be free of past controversy and antagonisms. Nixon surmounted those problems in 1968, but Dole did not in 1996. Voters are attracted by fresh faces who display no wounds. The late Republican National Chairman Lee Atwater once told me that Senator Phil Gramm of Texas could never be nominated "because he flunks the likability test. Nobody can be elected as president if he's not likable." "What about Nixon?" I asked. "Always an exception," responded Atwater.

- The nominee *should* be able to attract voters who spurned the Republican presidential candidate in 1992 and 1996—women, minority groups, young people, union members—while retaining the Republican base. That goal is an attempt to reconstruct the landslide Reagan majorities.

Only one prospective Republican candidate for 2000 seemed to pass *all* those tests: Governor George W. Bush of Texas. The name was an immeasurable help. In the years of Bill Clinton's presidency, the senior George Bush had been transformed from the despised loser of 1992 to a venerated party elder, so popular with American voters that in 1998 they told poll takers they would elect him, not Clinton, if they had to do it over again (though the same voters said they still would prefer Clinton over Dole).

•   •   •

The arrival of George Walker Bush at this lofty station at age fifty-three could hardly have been expected four or five years earlier and would have defied belief only a few years before that.

His political career seemed dead on arrival in 1978, when as a thirty-two-year-old hard-drinking, newly married small oil driller, he ran for Congress from the staunchly conservative Midland-Odessa district in West Texas. His opponent was conservative Democrat Kent Hance, a prototypical southern good ol' boy state legislator who campaigned as a "conservative Democrat" against "liberal Republican Bush."

Hance's television commercials depicted the Democratic candidate as a home-grown product of the Lubbock, Texas, public schools and the state-supported Texas Tech University, running against an export from eastern boarding schools, Yale College, and Harvard Business School. Though badly outspent by Bush, Hance won comfortably. (In his second term in Congress, he would defy Democratic leaders to co-sponsor President Reagan's tax cut bill, and a few years later, he became a Republican.)

George W. Bush returned to running his less than successful drilling company in West Texas. It hardly seemed possible that he would ever again run for public office in the wake of his spotty performance of 1978. Nobody could appreciate it at the time, but the first small step toward his reentry into politics occurred in 1979 when his father began a bid for the presidency that generated mostly laughter in the Republican establishment.

Despite an abundant résumé (two terms as a congressman from Houston, CIA director, ambassador to the UN, envoy to China and Republican national chairman), the senior George Bush's career in elective politics seemed to have ended back in 1970 when, for the second time, he was defeated as a U.S. Senate candidate in Texas. Bush was dead last in the early 1980 GOP presidential polls against an all-star field including Ronald Reagan (former governor of California), John Connally (former governor of Texas and former secretary of the treasury), Howard Baker (Senate minority leader), Senator Bob Dole, and Representatives John Anderson and Phil Crane. Bush called himself the "asterisk candidate," referring to the fact that an asterisk following his name signified that poll takers found no support at all for him.

But the Bush candidacy beat the odds, rising to the level of front-runner Reagan's biggest challenger, as all the other contenders were found wanting. When he upset Reagan in the Iowa caucuses, he set the wheels in motion to garner the vice-presidential nomination on the eventual winning ticket.

When Vice President Bush geared up to run for president in the 1988 election, his eldest son temporarily returned to politics. Young George W. moved his family to Washington to help in his father's campaign—but not in a role that would recommend him as a prospect for higher office.

The son was cast as his father's Washington-based enforcer, and he took that role seriously. "If someone jumped on my old man, I was jumping back," he has recalled. "I was a fierce warrior for George Bush." The targets of the "jumping" included Albert Hunt, then the Washington bureau chief of *The Wall Street Journal.* In a survey of political pundits by *Washingtonian* magazine in April 1986, Hunt had predicted that Republicans in 1988 would nominate Representative Jack Kemp of New York for president and Senator Richard Lugar of Indiana for vice president. Shortly after, in Dallas, George W. Bush encountered Hunt, his wife (the television journalist Judy Woodruff), and their four-year-old son lunching in a Mexican restaurant and "jumped" him. "You f——ing son of a bitch," said Bush (according to Hunt). "I saw what you wrote. We're not going to forget this."

Hunt thought that Bush had been drinking, and indeed, later that year George W. went on the wagon (on the morning after his fortieth birthday) because he thought it was interfering with his family and professional life. (In 1999, when the incident was brought to Bush's attention, he did not recall what was said but called Hunt with an apology.)

Nevertheless, Bush's infrequent public contacts continued to suggest more of an immature smart aleck than a political professional carefully choosing his words. At the 1988 Republican convention in Houston that nominated George Bush for president, David Fink of *The Hartford Courant* asked the son what he and his father talked about when they weren't talking politics. The one-word answer: an obscene description of women. A shocked Fink later wrote that that remark was the younger Bush's "good ol' boy version of charm."

A year after his father's election as president, George W. moved to Dallas and invested $600,000 ($500,000 of it borrowed money) for a 1.8 percent share of the Texas Rangers baseball team and the post of its managing director, an arrangement facilitated by the fact that the seller of the team was Eddie Chiles, a Texas businessman who had been a long-time supporter of the elder Bush. As managing director of the Rangers, Bush directed construction of the team's spectacular home, The Ballpark at Arlington, financed by a one-half-cent sales tax increase approved by a referendum of Arlington voters. The view of him in the baseball world was summed up by an executive of another team who had been active in Republican politics. "He was smart, and I thought he was a good salesman. But he was a little cocky, a little arrogant in dealing with other people. It never occurred to me that he was a future president of the United States."

Nevertheless, the change to this high-profile position from the obscurity of his little oil firm encouraged his father's friends to start talking to him about trying elective politics again. Republican party chairman Lee Atwater alerted friends in Texas to support him for governor in 1990, but that was too much, too soon for Bush, particularly since he would have been thrown into a fierce, multicandidate Republican primary election. Instead, he enjoyed lavish, favorable publicity as the man who built The Ballpark at Arlington while he slowly and quietly built Republican contacts around the state under the guidance of Dallas businessman Jim Francis and Austin-based political consultant Karl Rove.

In 1994, Bush was ready, and so was the Texas GOP, whose leaders anointed him as the nominee early and without serious opposition. Democratic Governor Ann Richards, a battle-hardened career politician, was popular and a fabulously tough campaigner. Her strategy was to bait Bush, calling him "Shrub" and a "jerk," saying he would not be running for governor if his name were "George Walker" and accusing him, falsely, of serial business failures. Her expectation was that given his volatile reputation, George W. would blow. He didn't.

Instead, the Bush campaign's strategy was to "kill her with kindness." The candidate never retaliated in kind, proving a cool warrior and an effective, if less than exciting, campaigner who focused on and never strayed from a four-point program: welfare reform, tort reform, more local school control, tougher juvenile justice. In rural areas that had never supported a Republican, he declared: "Do not judge me as a Republican. Judge me as a conservative."

His only unintended departure from script came in an interview when he asserted his creed as a born-again Christian: he believed his acceptance of Christ as a personal savior was the path to heaven. Democrats generated a whispering campaign that he was a narrow-minded, anti-Jewish bigot.

To no avail. Bush's disciplined campaign for governor was rewarded with 54 percent of the vote. And his investment in the Texas Rangers had brought him more than just favorable publicity; it made him a rich man. Selling his share of the team following his election as governor, he cashed in for $14.9 million (another $2 million was expected after final accounting).

• • •

In 1995, George W. Bush entered the governor's office in Austin appearing to be more southern, more conservative, and a lot more of a regular guy than his father—indeed more like his feisty, widely beloved mother. But from the beginning, he seemed to repeat his father's grievous error of trying to raise taxes after promising that he would not.

He proposed $1 billion in property tax relief, to be paid for by closing the loophole that permitted some of the state's biggest businesses—including many major newspapers—to escape the Texas franchise tax through limited partnerships. Conservative Republicans bitterly opposed the new governor's program, noting grimly that the apple never falls far from the tree.

But George W. proved that in politics, it's sometimes better to be lucky than good. A coalition of conservative Democrats and Republicans in the legislature killed the tax increase but retained the $1 billion property tax relief. What's more, a resurgent Texas economy yielded so much revenue that it was unnecessary for Bush to seek compensating sales tax increases, as Democrats predicted he would be forced to do.

In the governor's chair, Bush proved a surprisingly masterful politician. In contrast to the aloof Ann Richards, he strolled the floors of the state Senate and House, slapping backs, trading jokes, and seeking support. He kept the support of the full range of Republicans, while gaining that of influential Democrats. Austin lobbyist George Christian, who for the previous forty years was a confidant of such establishment Democrats as Lyndon Johnson and Lloyd Bentsen, became a Bush admirer. So did the highly influential Democratic lieutenant governor, Bob Bullock, whose relationship with Governor Richards had been tenuous. (In Texas, the lieutenant governor, who presides over the Senate, is one of the most powerful politicians in the state.) Bullock was retiring from politics at the end of his term, but he endorsed Bush for reelection in 1998—the first time he had ever backed a Republican.

The Texas governorship is weak, having been diluted in strength by post–Civil War Democrats to make sure no Republican carpetbagger had too much power. So Bush's early record of accomplishment was less substantial than his popularity.

By 1997, it was so clear that Bush would be reelected in a landslide in 1998 that Democratic strategists in Austin seriously talked about not contesting the governorship so that the governor's expected big victory would not sweep the entire ticket for the GOP—good advice, it turned out, that was not accepted.

Bush-for-president talk was rampant well before his first term for governor was completed.

• • •

Would the Bush magic travel well? His managers handled him carefully, routinely rejecting invitations for national television interviews and limiting his national exposure. The wisdom of that rigid discipline was demonstrated best when it broke down, as it did when he accepted an invitation to the party's biennial midwestern regional conference at Indianapolis in late August 1997. Whether or not his Texas staff fully understood it, this event was the first "cattle show" of the 2000 election cycle.

The expectations were overwhelming, but the results were disappointing. Bush had less contact with the delegates in Indianapolis than any other prospective presidential candidate, he did not meet the press, and the speech he delivered to the conference's showcase Saturday night dinner was a lackluster account of the previous Texas legislative session. He did not look ready for prime time, and it was a signal to his advisers to stay away from similar cattle calls as he prepared for his 1998 reelection.

That election was a laugher and, as Democrats had feared, Bush's coattails proved broad, electing all the Republican statewide candidates for the first time in Texas history—including the lieutenant governor, guaranteeing that the party would retain the governorship if Bush went to Washington. He had run extraordinarily well with all the voter groups that had been rejecting his party elsewhere: women, young people, Hispanics, even African Americans.

By the day of the election, George W. Bush was clearly anointed as the party's choice for 2000 by the Republican establishment: members of the Republican National Committee, major contributors in the Team 100, his fellow governors, members of Congress, local party leaders across the country. Unbelievably, the 2000 nomination was his to lose. But what did he stand for, and what kind of campaign would he run?

• • •

Bush would not emerge as a full-blown presidential candidate until the state legislative session ended on May 31, 1999. But his operatives had been at work preparing the way even before the 1998 election, and it was clear what was ahead:

- Bush would be a dependably conservative candidate—anti-abortion, pro–school choice, pro–tax cut, anti–big government.

- He would soft-pedal issues, especially abortion, that antagonized the country club wing of the party as he sought to hold together the Republican coalition. Yet he kept social conservatives happy in his 1999 legislative session, mainly by guiding an abortion parental consent bill through the legislature.
- Learning by bad example from the 1996 Dole campaign, the Bush effort would be lean on staff and long on television spending.
- His father's political retainers, eager to take part in a Bush restoration, would not be part of the son's team. It was made clear early that their support was welcome—but their presence was not.
- His last legislation was closely watched by political reporters sent to Austin by *The New York Times* and the *Washington Post* as well as network television. He came through with an impressive performance, getting most, though not all, of the things he wanted—and keeping off his desk some things he did not want. It looked as if Bush would have to sign a hate-crimes bill, inspired by the racist murder of a black man in Jasper, Texas, but that would not have pleased social conservatives. So the governor quietly kept the bill bottled up in committee.
- After the legislative session, his unveiling in Iowa as a presidential candidate went off without a mistake.

It was an impressive start. Yet no Republican since General Dwight D. Eisenhower in 1952 had been elected president on his first try. Bush had a steep learning curve, especially on foreign affairs, as was evident in the fact that in his early weeks on the campaign stump, he mistook Slovakia for Slovenia. Fortunately for him, nobody seemed to care much.

His early comments on the war of Yugoslavia were uninformed and generally unimpressive. In his behalf, a spokesman delivered a soggy finesse: "He believes that is a decision for the commander in chief who has the military and intelligence information." On the next day, Bush spoke for himself but was not much more decisive: "My worry is the worry of a lot of people I've heard from in Texas and that is, will the air strikes achieve the President's stated mission of bringing [Yugoslav President Slobodan] Milosevic back to the peace table. And if not, what next?" But ten days later, he became markedly more hawkish: "Now that we're in it, we ought to plan to win, even if that means ground troops." At a point where a substantial Republican majority was against escalating the war, their anointed leader was going in the opposite direction.

Bush's wobbling was not even close to George Romney's disastrous performance three decades earlier, when he blundered into saying that he had been "brainwashed" on a trip to Vietnam. Still, the question was whispered: Would he follow Romney's course in the 1968 race and fail to navigate this strange territory? Could too much be expected of George W. Bush?

Much was expected of him by the GOP's power structure—not merely the state chairmen and national committee members but the shadow hierarchy of Washington lobbyists who came from the ranks of party functionaries and still dabbled in Republican affairs. Typical was former national chairman Haley Barbour, a country lawyer from Yazoo City, Mississippi, who was now a seven-figure-a-year Washington lobbyist. Notoriously cautious, Barbour gave out a clear signal when he unexpectedly turned up in Austin in early 1999 as one of the ten-member Bush-for-president exploratory committee.

But were Barbour and his fellow Republican establishmentarians engaging in wishful thinking in their gamble that the unseasoned Bush could survive this ordeal? The danger lay in the lack of a fallback candidate should the anointed one fail. When Romney dropped the baton in the autumn of 1967, former Vice President Richard M. Nixon—seasoned and ready—was there to pick it up. There was no Nixon ready in 1999.

But there were opponents of the anointment of George W. Bush, angry enough to threaten to leave the party or even actually leave.

• • •

Robert C. Smith, a forty-nine-year-old former high school civics teacher, was elected to the U.S. Senate from New Hampshire in 1990 after having served three terms in the House of Representatives. Tall (six feet, six inches) and stout (referred to as "Lumpy" behind his back in the Republican cloakroom), Smith was a stolid, unbending conservative known for his tenacious opposition to abortion and a fruitless effort to find surviving American prisoners of war in Communist Vietnam.

If thought a little eccentric, he was popular enough among his fellow Republican senators that in the fall of 1996, several of them (including Senator William Cohen of Maine, who in a few weeks would be named by President Clinton as his third secretary of defense) went to New Hampshire to campaign for Smith in a tough battle for reelection. On election night, the television networks declared him defeated based on exit polls skewed by excessive concentration on urban areas. On the next morning, the final returns showed he had barely survived—hardly the kind of showing that would generally propel someone into national politics.

But that was precisely what happened. To everyone's surprise, in January 1999, Bob Smith declared himself to be a candidate for president—without money, organization, or much popular support. He explained: "I do identify with Jimmy Stewart in the movie *Mr. Smith Goes to Washington*. He was good person who took on the special interests and the power brokers. I believe in that, I know it might sound simplistic." But this Mr. Smith got nowhere. His campaign could not even break the 1 percent mark in his own state of New Hampshire, much less nationally, and could generate neither attention nor respect.

Six months later, Smith abandoned not only his race for the Republican presidential nomination but also his lifelong party. When he let it be known that he was changing his Senate designation from Republican to Independent and was considering becoming the presidential candidate of the U.S. Taxpayers party, Republican National chairman Jim Nicholson and New Hampshire chairman Steve Dunfrey assailed him. Taking leave of the GOP on the Senate floor, Smith said that he had watched the Jimmy Stewart movie again and declared: "I've come to the cold realization that the Republican party is more interested in winning elections than supporting the principles of its platform." Specifically, he said the party was abandoning its anti-abortion and pro-gun platform planks. (A few weeks later, perhaps reacting to the assemblage of oddballs and extremists gathered under the Taxpayers banner, Smith also left that party. By the end of October he had pulled out of the race and was mulling a return to the GOP.

During his brief run nobody thought that Smith posed

much of a threat to the party. Much more worrisome was
the reaction among the other GOP presidential contenders.
Nicholson and Dunfrey's sharp criticism was assailed by
Steve Forbes, Gary Bauer, and Pat Buchanan. Indeed, Buchanan did what he had refused to do in 1996 against Bob
Dole, despite the pleading of his rank-and-file supporters to
do so, and run as an independent himself. Shortly before
Smith bolted, Buchanan told me: "I have not gone to a meeting where someone has not got up and asked me to leave the
Republican party and go third party." Now he said that he
would contest the nomination of Ross Perot's Reform party,
and that was worrisome for the GOP. Bob Smith and the
U.S. Taxpayers party was one thing. Pat Buchanan and the
Reform party (with its $12.5 million in federal funds guaran-
teed under the election law, based on Perot's vote-getting in
1996) was quite another.

Buchanan declared that the test of whether he would join
Smith in apostasy was whether he concluded, as he now suspected, that the nomination had been rigged for George W.
Bush. By September, that suspicion had hardened into cer-
tainty, as Buchanan signaled he would seek the Reform party
nomination, a step he finally took on October 25.

Buchanan really was protesting Bush's anointment when
he praised Smith. So were Forbes and Bauer. Indeed, Smith's
precipitous departure from the party had the same root as
Buchanan's bolt.

They were protesting not only that Bush had wrapped up
the organization, but that the anointed candidate might be
shaky on the conservative agenda. True, on every issue that I
have discussed, the governor was sound. What worried the
proponents of the revolution was the "mood music" accom-
panying Bush as he proclaimed "compassionate conser-

vatism" and "a different role for government" to cooperate with churches and charities to help the underclass. These were laudable goals. But the skeptics wondered whether they would take precedence over renewing the revolution.

Thoughtful Republicans worry about a fate in some ways worse than defeat in 2000: the party's first simultaneous control of the White House and both houses of Congress since 1953–1954, with the same outcome as then. Much of the misery Republicans experienced in subsequent years can be traced to the vapid quality of the first two Eisenhower years. If a new Bush administration were to repeat those mistakes, the impact on the party would be calamitous.

Therein lies the greatest danger of anointment, lacking a true contest for the nomination. It deprives the party of seeing who can emerge the best and who can best embody the principles that unite the party's rank and file.

It can be a recipe for disaster in either of two outcomes:

- If the anointed candidate falls along the primary trail, the ensuing free-for-all could result in an unsatisfactory conclusion.
- If the anointed candidate is nominated as planned, he may prove unready and be a desperate disappointment in the general election campaign.

The risk in early anointment was pointed up quickly in late summer 1999 when Governor Bush stumbled in handling rumors—but no specific allegations—that he had used cocaine and other illegal drugs as a young man. While volunteering that he had ended a drinking problem and that he always had been faithful to his wife, he refused to answer drug questions.

But on August 18, veteran *Dallas Morning News* reporter Sam Attlesey asked him privately whether he as president would insist on current FBI standards that White House employees cannot have used drugs in the past seven years. He replied yes and that he could pass the test. When the newspaper the next morning headlined that Bush asserted he had not used illegal drugs in seven years, Bush asserted he could pass the fifteen-year test set by his father when he became president in 1989. That self-described the governor as drug free back to 1974, when he was twenty-eight years old, but he refused to say more in anticipation it would open the floodgate of more personal questions based on rumor and speculation.

The rookie presidential candidate stumbled through the process, and Democratic political operatives were euphoric. Clinton hit-man James Carville rejoiced to friends that if Bush stumbled here, the Republicans were left without a credible candidate for 2000. Republicans admitted that Carville might be all too correct. The news media firestorm about the unanswered "cocaine question" subsided in late August, but Republicans worried about how and when it would be revived.

● ● ●

The early anointment of George W. Bush is not only a tremendous gamble for the Republicans but a decision that minimizes—in truth neglects—what the Republican party needs to do to survive in the new century. The party leaders lining up behind Bush are placing all hope on an untried champion who may—or may not—share the philosophy needed to transform the government. The months ahead will show whether this gamble will pay off.

The Courage
to Be Republicans

The performances honored by Senator John F. Kennedy in his 1956 book, *Profiles in Courage,* are essentially isolated political acts running against the tide and counter to the individual's self-interest. The most memorable for me was the unexpected vote in 1868 by Republican Senator Edmund Gibson Ross of Kansas against conviction of the impeached President Andrew Johnson, so that Johnson survived removal from office by just one vote short of the necessary two-thirds Senate majority. That made Ross a pariah in the Republican party and effectively ended his political career. A close second, Kennedy's most controversial example, was the shocking criticism of the Nuremberg war crimes trials by Senator Robert A. Taft of Ohio, "Mr. Republican" of his day. Universally condemned, Taft's posture may well have doomed his chances for the presidential nomination in 1948 and 1952.

The courage to be a Republican in 2000 requires something of Edmund Ross's or Robert A. Taft's willingness to charge full speed into the teeth of the conventional wisdom and political correctness. But it is also something quite different. Such courage is not an isolated act or one that necessarily means the end of a political career. It does mean the determination to stand by what the Republican party has come to mean, no matter if it collides with the caution and stop signals flashed by polls and focus groups.

The simple yet demanding nature of this kind of courage occurred to me the Friday night before the Memorial Day weekend of 1999, when I appeared on CNN's *Crossfire* with David Corn, the Washington editor of *The Nation* and a bright, young, left-wing journalist. The broadcast followed another dismal stretch for the Republicans controlling Congress that had become all too frequent since the GOP's takeover in the 1994 elections.

It had begun a month earlier in the Senate, when Majority Leader Trent Lott bowed to Democratic demands to debate previously unscheduled gun control measures in reaction to the shootings at Columbine High School in Littleton, Colorado, in which thirteen students and a teacher were shot to death by two student gunmen. Lott agreed to call up a juvenile justice bill and open it up for gun amendments within two weeks—too short a period for careful preparation.

When a Democratic package of gun measures was voted down by a 51–47 vote, largely along party lines, the news media erupted in outrage that the Republicans were bowing to the dictates of the National Rifle Association. Several Republican senators, led by presidential hopeful John McCain, were also outraged—not by the substance of the issue but the news media's reaction—and won reconsideration of the vote. A series of Republican retreats culminated ten days later in a vote on the original Democratic proposals that had been rejected. That resulted in a 50–50 vote, giving the probable Democratic presidential nominee for 2000—Vice President Al Gore—the opportunity for a much publicized tie-breaking vote.

In the House, rookie Speaker Dennis Hastert accepted nearly everything in the Senate Democratic package but delayed taking it up until after Memorial Day. The week before the holiday was supposed to be occupied with passing three appropriations bills and the Defense Department's authorization. Hastert, having promised to "make the trains run on time," considered it a point of principle to pass these appropriations on schedule for the first time since the Republicans took over Congress and not to worry about any kind of "revolution" to change the face of government.

But a funny thing happened on the way to the railroad station: the trains didn't run at all. The Agriculture Department's appropriations bill was loaded with additional spending. The indomitable Representative Tom Coburn of Oklahoma, representing angry backbench Republican conservatives, prepared more than a hundred amendments to cut the amount of money for the farmers. The Republican leadership had to take the bill off the floor. On the Defense bill, Hastert had promised the White House not to vote on an amendment setting a deadline on financing of the war in Kosovo. Rank-and-file Republicans caused so much trouble that this bill had to be taken off the floor as well.

Nor were the other two appropriations bills passed that week. In fact, nothing was done. Hastert's proposition had been that if the bills were passed, the House would get the whole week off after Memorial Day instead of going back to work on Tuesday, June 1, as originally scheduled. But in the permissive and lax climate prevailing, the congressmen gave themselves the week off even though they had done nothing. The House adjourned on Thursday, May 27, not to return for ten days.

On *Crossfire* the next night, Corn asked the guest—Representative David Dreier of California, the chairman of the House Rules Committee and a high-ranking member of the Republican leadership—when the House would pass gun control, as well as a higher minimum wage, campaign finance reform, and a "patients' bill of rights" reforming health maintenance organizations. Dreier hastily assured the leftist journalist that all of these would be taken up in due time.

But I noted to Corn that his agenda consisted solely of Democratic proposals. What about the *Republican* agenda? What about, say, privatization of Social Security? Corn snickered. He would be more than pleased, he replied, if the GOP turned to the right and guaranteed a Democratic triumph in 2000.

Is that the correct equation? Would the courage to be Republicans consign the party to the dust bin in history, ensuring for it the same fate as Edmund Ross and Robert A. Taft?

• • •

I don't think so. Actually, even if a collective Republican profile in courage were to prove fatal, the alternative is even worse. But I don't equate courage with suicide. For Republicans to stand by their principles does not condemn them to a kamikaze bombing raid.

The courage to be a Republican is the courage to stand for principles, which can be embodied in various government or legislative proposals. The overriding basis for these principles is the old-fashioned "republican virtue" on which the United States government was founded. That does not constitute a rejection of government's proper role but stresses the paramount importance of the individual. For Republicans approaching the millennial election, there are underlying principles that they should be proud to champion:

Tax Reform. The *courage* to scrap the Internal Revenue Code even though the alternative system will be savaged as favoring the rich against the poor.

Diminished Government. The *courage* to cut back on the bloated federal Leviathan, even though the popular Education Department and the special-interest favored National Endowment for the Arts would be endangered.

Enlightened Nationalism. The *courage* to stand for a strong national defense, free trade, and a nonbelligerent foreign policy while averting the temptation to serve as policeman for the entire world.

Equal Rights. The *courage* to stand against racial quotas and for educational choice, amid accusations of racism.

Government Reform. The *courage* to stand for term limits and campaign finance reform, even though in the short run they may seem to be to the disadvantage of the Republican party.

Privatized Social Security. The *courage* to end, not mend, the existing Social Security system for the future, so that the protracted Ponzi scheme is replaced by a privatized pension plan.

Right to Life. The *courage* to oppose abortion as a moral question, even at the risk of losing Republican supporters.

Individual Freedom. The *courage* to return governmental emphasis to the freedom of the individual to do the unwise—to spend his own money as he wishes, to own guns, even to smoke cigarettes.

This is not the agenda that will come out of the polls and focus groups that Republican politicians are as obsessed about as Bill Clinton is. But it is close to the heart of the GOP, and I believe it is the surest way for any Republican to be elected president in 2000.

• • •

Why are Republicans so reluctant to embrace this agenda? Is it simple cowardice? Not exactly. Rather, the fear of losing—losing votes, losing their majority, ultimately losing their seats in Congress—haunts them.

As a basketball buff who has watched thousands of basketball games over the last half century, I am reminded by these Republicans in Congress of teams that, instead of playing to win, have played not to lose. Often basketball teams with superior talent were defeated because they did not play to win. Let me cite two examples.

In the 1977 National Basketball Association finals, the Philadelphia 76ers with the inimitable Julius (Dr. J) Erving were heavily favored against the Portland Trailblazers. The Sixers won the first two games in Philadelphia and headed west to Oregon with a 2–0 edge in the best-of-seven series—the kind of lead that usually proves insurmountable. But I sensed something wrong with Dr. J and his teammates once they arrived in Portland. They were cautious, fearful of making mistakes, playing not to lose. The Trailblazers won four straight and the championship.

In the 1999 National Collegiate Athletic Association championship, Duke University entered the final game against an underdog University of Connecticut team after a dream season in which they lost only one game at the very beginning of the year and would be rated as one of the greatest college teams of all time—if, that is, they won the national title. The pressure to win was manifest, and I saw those manifest signs of playing not to lose. This was not the Duke team that had played with such reckless abandon all year (including two runaway wins against my beloved and very good University of Maryland team), but a team that was cautious, timid, spooked. Connecticut won the national championship.

In a sense, then, Republicans need the courage to play to win.

•   •   •

They also need the courage to avoid a competition with Democrats that accepts the merits of big government and reduces the debate to which party can more efficiently run the government. It is an argument that the Republicans can never win.

Yet it is an argument that many conservatives pursue, and with the fading of the Gingrich revolution, it has become an underlying premise guiding the Republican congressional leadership. The founding document of this movement was "What Ails Conservatism," an essay published in *The Wall Street Journal* on September 15, 1997, and written by William Kristol and his colleague on *The Weekly Standard*, David Brooks. What ails the Republican party, they concluded, was its attack on big government.

The Kristol-Brooks thesis was that "an American political movement's highest goal can't be protecting citizens from their own government" and that "a conservatism that organizes citizens' resentments rather than informing their hopes will always fall short of fundamental victory." Astonishingly, they asked: "How can Americans love their nation and hate its government?" Their question unwittingly validated Bill Clinton's deplorable insinuation that it was criticism of government that spawned the terrorist bombing of the Oklahoma City federal building in 1995. The best answer was provided by Thomas Paine in *Common Sense*, when he said, "Government even in its best state is but a necessary evil; in its worst state an intolerable one."

Kristol and Brooks traced their thesis back to the big-government doctrines of conservative founding father Alexander Hamilton, and Senator Phil Gramm of Texas was quickly able to translate the historical reference to modern terms. A native Georgian, Gramm had been born and raised a Democrat dedicated to the small-government doctrines of Thomas Jefferson and was first elected to Congress as a Democrat but crossed the aisle to become a Republican in 1982. Although today's Democrats still pay lip-service to the Jeffersonian ideals, they long ago ignored his strictures about the "degeneracy of government." But have the Republicans adopted the abandoned Jefferson?

That would take courage. After the Kristol-Brooks essay was published, Gramm told me that Hamilton's views are "anachronistic," and added this: "We are Jeffersonians. The longer I live the more convinced I am that there are only two ideas in history: government and freedom. When government is the answer, the Democrats are in the ascendancy. When freedom is the answer, we are in the ascendancy."

Nearly two years later, in *The Weekly Standard* of August 2, 1999, David Brooks quoted, a little triumphantly, a recent speech by George W. Bush attacking the "destructive mindset: the idea that if government would only get out of our way, all our problems will be solved." Brooks used Bush's address as a starting point for his argument that "vehement anti-government thinking" in the Republican party "crested" in 1995 prior to the government shutdown and "is now in retreat." In 1999, Bush did not go as far as the Kristol-Brooks thesis of 1997, but close enough to question the courage of the party to be Jeffersonian.

• • •

What a Republican is and, indeed, what a conservative is, has changed over the past 150 years. The issues are different, and so is the country. But I believe the contrasting models for the GOP truly go back to the turn of the last century, models offered by two imposing figures: Theodore Roosevelt of New York and Thomas Brackett Reed of Maine.

Teddy Roosevelt has become so universally a recognized icon of the Grand Old Party that he now approaches Abraham Lincoln in the level of veneration among all kinds of Republicans. Tom Reed is nearly forgotten. Roosevelt's photograph is found in the offices of literally hundreds of prominent Republicans; Reed's in none.

As a young boy growing up in a liberal Republican household, I looked to TR as one of my personal heroes— the puny, sickly youth who became an amateur boxer, a big-game hunter, and a sometime cowboy. The hero who stormed up San Juan Hill leading his Rough Riders in the Spanish-American War was the first American president to be a world figure, sending the Great White Fleet around the world and negotiating the Russo-Japanese peace settlement at Portsmouth, New Hampshire. He was the trustbuster, the leading "progressive" Republican, and the friend of the working man.

Tom Reed? I knew him only as a not very attractive bit player in the history books, the "Czar Reed" who exercised dictatorial rule as Speaker of the House of Representatives in the 1890s, the Old Guard Republican with the bay window caricatured in the famous Nast cartoons.

Not much of a contest. But let's look closer.

Roosevelt: Imperialist (he called it "expansionist") who boomed, "We are a conquering race!" in justifying domination over lesser breeds; big spender; advocate of growing and intrusive government; advocate of higher taxes (and founding father of the onerous inheritance tax). And the father of the federal police state. When Congress refused to vote appropriations for new Justice Department investigators, TR managed to evade the legislative will and launched the Bureau of Investigation (later the FBI) on his own authority—the beginning of federal agencies threatening personal freedom. He is the real model for the Kristol-Brooks brand of conservatism. Not surprisingly, amateur historian Roosevelt regarded Jefferson as one of the nation's worst presidents.

Reed: Advocate of low taxes, limited government, and personal freedom, with the courage to be anti-imperialist challenging the popular will at the time of the Spanish-American War. An imperialist America made him heartsick—sick of politics, sick of Washington.

More than sixty years later, in her book *The Proud Tower*, the historian Barbara Tuchman wrote: "Reed's whole life was in Congress, in politics, in the exercise of representative government, with the qualification that for him it had to be exercised toward an end that he believed in." To his secretary, Speaker Reed wrote, "I have tried, perhaps not always successfully, to make the acts of my public life accord with my conscience and I cannot now do this thing." The greatest legislator of his day stunned the political world by retiring from public life in April 1899, at age fifty-nine.

What would Reed have thought of the Republicans of a century later? Not much, I fear. Some of Reed's issues are out of date; others are not. But the courage and commitment to freedom and old-fashioned republican virtue of Tom Reed can guide Republicans on the way to 2000.

The question: will they take it?

Index